Y0-DCF-519

DATE DUE

NO 14 '97	JE 2 7 '08		
DE 19 '97	DE 19 '08		
AP 20 '98	JE 8 '17		
MY 27 '98	JY 27 '11		
NO 3 '98	NO 4 '17		
	JE 8 '15		
	E 17 '19		
AP 25 '99			
MY 27 '99			
NO 30 '99			
DE 2 '00			
AP			

WI'   ON

A   S E L F   ? O G R A M

 **Mosby**
Consumer Health Division

First Edition

Special thanks to clinical consultants:

Wayne J. Katon, M.D.
Professor of Psychiatry
University of Washington Medical School
Seattle, Washington

Jeanne Miranda, Ph.D.
Department of Psychiatry
San Francisco General Hospital
San Francisco, California

© 1996 Mosby-Yearbook, Inc.

Printed in the United States of America

Mosby-Yearbook, Inc.
11830 Westline Industrial Dr.
St. Louis, MO 63146
1-800-433-3803

ISBN 0-8151-9595-8 / 26513

Printed on recycled paper.

FOREWORD

Living well with any mental illness requires a unique combination of skills. First, it involves learning as much as you can about your problem—everything from what's causing the condition to how different medications work. Next, it takes time and effort to form a solid partnership with members of your health care team. This includes the doctors, nurses, therapists, and pharmacists who will be working with you. Being an active partner in mental health care means that you prepare for your visits, you actively seek answers to questions, and you understand treatment recommendations.

Self-management of your condition also requires that you learn how to track and monitor your progress. You will recognize signs that signal the need to see your doctor, and you will learn what you can handle yourself.

These are important skills in caring for any medical condition. There's something else that determines much of how you feel. It's the lifestyle choices you make every day in nutrition, appropriate physical activity, and stress-management. These changes start with a willingness to change, a can-do attitude, and a long-range perspective.

In the pages ahead, you'll find helpful information in all of these areas.

For almost 100 years, the Mosby company has provided your doctors, nurses, and allied health professionals with the latest information and advances in medicine. We're proud now to bring these same quality resources to help you gain the necessary knowledge, skills, and support for the best of health.

Mark J. Tager, M.D.

Mark J. Tager, M.D.
Medical Director, Mosby-Consumer Health, Inc.

TABLE OF CONTENTS

INTRODUCTION

All of us suffer the "blues" from time to time. In fact, feeling down is a normal and even healthy reaction to loss and stress. With time, these feelings usually pass. However, for some people, feelings of sadness, hopelessness, and heaviness go on and on. These people feel powerless over the intense despair that surrounds them. They suffer from a medical condition called depression.

Depression is so common that doctors call it the common cold of mental illness. According to the U.S. Department of Health and Human Services, about one in 20 people—more than 11 million of us—suffer from depression every year. For reasons doctors don't quite understand, women suffer depression twice as often as men.

Depression can affect anyone. It can also take several different forms. These are called mood disorders. If you or someone you know suffers from a mood disorder, it may help you to know that many well-known and respected people throughout history have suffered from them too. King Saul of biblical fame, Abraham Lincoln, Winston Churchill, Theodore Roosevelt, Leo Tolstoy, Virginia Woolfe, and Ernest Hemingway, among many others, suffered from what Churchill called "the black dog" of depression.

The good news is that depression is a treatable medical illness. Unfortunately, many people are uncomfortable asking for help for a mental problem. People may not ask for help because they feel they should just snap out of it. Others feel they should be depressed because something sad happened to them. In fact, experts estimate that only one in three people who suffer from depression seeks help. Unfortunately, this leads to unnecessary suffering. Depression is not a weakness or character flaw. It is a medical illness just like diabetes, high blood pressure, or heart disease. And it can be treated. Treatment can reduce the pain and suffering of depression. Successful treatment can remove all of the symptoms of depression and allow you to return to your normal life. As with other health problems, the sooner you get the right treatment, the sooner you'll start to feel better.

This book can be a big part of your treatment. You'll learn about:

- different types of mood disorders, including possible causes and risk factors

- signs and symptoms of mood disorders

- how doctors diagnose mood disorders

- which treatments are available

- how to work with your health care team to get the most from your treatment

- lifestyle changes you can make to help relieve your depression

You don't have to let depression ruin your self-esteem, disrupt your relationships, or get in the way of work and other important parts of your life. Help *is* available. Working with your health care team and reading this book are big steps toward feeling better and living depression-free.

How to Use This Book

Use this book almost any way you like. You don't have to read it straight through—you can pick and choose sections that seem important to you today and go back to others later.

Each section starts by listing the topics it covers. You'll also find *terms* in bold italic type throughout the text, which are defined in the **Glossary** on pp. 88–92. You may want to look over that section before you start to read this book. This way you'll know some of the terms you will see. Or feel free to look them up as they come up in your reading.

SECTION I: UNDERSTANDING MOOD DISORDERS

Knowing more about mood disorders can help you feel less worried and anxious about the mood disorder you or someone you care about may have. If you are depressed, it helps to know that there are real reasons for your feelings that can be treated. In this section, we'll talk about:

- What is a mood disorder?
- What are the types of mood disorders?
- What causes mood disorders?
- Who's at risk for mood disorders?

WHAT IS A MOOD DISORDER?

The term ***mood disorder*** refers to periods of extreme changes in mood that go beyond normal feelings about daily events. This book covers the most common types of mood disorders:

- major depressive disorder

- bipolar disorder

- dysthymia

- seasonal affective disorder (SAD)

All of these disorders involve the condition of ***depression***.

There is a big difference between normal depression and the depression that can happen with any of these mood disorders. Some depression is a normal response to certain life events, such as a major letdown or loss. Mood disorders involve changes in emotion, thinking, and behavior that are *more severe* and *longer lasting* than normal reactions to life's ups and downs.

There are also different degrees of mood disorders. Your depression may be mild, moderate, or severe. The degree of your mood disorder can make a big difference in the treatment plan that is best for you.

Everyone feels depression differently. Some complain mostly of physical symptoms. Others of changes in emotion (emotional symptoms) and thinking (cognitive symptoms). Most people with depression also have changes in behavior (behavioral symptoms). With all of these differences, it is important to seek professional advice if you feel you may have any type or degree of mood disorder.

TYPES OF MOOD DISORDERS

You may already have been told that you have a mood disorder. If so, you will want to know as much about it as you can to make the best choices about your treatment. If you feel you may have a mood disorder but have not seen a health care professional for a checkup, this section will give you an idea of the possible reasons for your depression.

Major Depressive Disorder

People with *major depression* describe it as living in a black hole, feeling dead, or being overcome with doom. When you're depressed, you may be overwhelmed by feelings of sadness and despair. Or you may feel nothing, empty, without any feelings. Many people with major depression have trouble paying attention or making decisions. Some feel anxious all the time. Without treatment, these feelings can go on for weeks, months, or even years.

Often, people with major depression lose interest in normally enjoyable activities. For instance, if you're a big baseball fan, you may suddenly not care about an upcoming World Series. If you're a parent, you may no longer be interested in your children. Activities, people, and issues that once were important are no longer meaningful. You view the world through gray-tinted glasses. Everything is bleak—your life, your future. You just don't feel the pleasure or interest in things you used to enjoy.

Depression affects the body, too. You may find you can't sleep or that you sleep too much. You may wake during the night or very early in the morning and be unable to go back to sleep. You may eat all the time or eat almost nothing at all. Sex may not interest you. You may have a wide range of little aches and pains, including heart palpitations and upset stomach, and you'll likely feel tired all the time. When you're depressed, your self-esteem may suffer from feeling worthless, helpless, and guilty. You may think over and over about your real and imagined failures, often making too much out of past little mistakes.

Doctors classify depression by degree: severe, moderate, or mild. You have severe depression if you have nearly all of the symptoms of depression and they keep you from doing your daily activities. Moderate

Symptoms of Major Depression

Physical:

- changes in appetite

- weight loss or weight gain

- changes in sleep pattern—sleeping little or too much in an irregular pattern

- excessive fatigue and feelings of tiredness

- decreased sexual drive

- pain—headaches, stomach pain, or other body aches

Emotional:

- apathy, irritability, or anxiety

- feelings of sadness, pessimism, or hopelessness

- feelings of worthlessness or excessive guilt

Cognitive:

- inability to think clearly or concentrate

- repeated thoughts about death or causing oneself harm; suicide attempts

Behavioral:

- loss of interest in usual activities

- boredom, no sense of humor

depression means you have many of the symptoms and they often keep you from doing the things you need to do. You have mild depression if you have some of the symptoms and it takes extra effort to do the things you need to do.

Experts say that if you have already gone through an *episode* of major depression, you have a 50 to 85 percent chance of having at least one more episode in your lifetime. Most people with major depression average between five and seven episodes over their lifetime. Sometimes episodes are separated by many years of feeling normal; other times the episodes tend to run in clusters.

Bipolar Disorder

Some people who have episodes of major depression may also swing to the other end of the emotional scale. They may have times of *hypomania* or the more severe state of *mania*. These are times of extreme excitement and activity. Doctors call these extreme mood swings *bipolar disorder* (or *manic depression*).

If you have bipolar disorder, sometimes you feel great, on top of the world, even though, at other times, you may feel angry or irritable. You'll likely talk more than normal, your thoughts coming so fast it's hard to express them. You'll be more active and need less sleep. The mania can make it hard to think. Your mind may be drawn to unimportant or minute details. You'll feel great about yourself and, in some cases, you may even have exaggerated ideas of your own importance. For instance, during a manic episode a person might think he or she is the only one who can save the community from some deadly threat.

One of the dangers of mania is that you're likely to make decisions and take action without thinking about the results. For instance, it's not unusual for someone in a manic state to make foolish business decisions, buy thousands of dollars' worth of unneeded items, or show an uncharacteristic increase in sexual activity. Some people become so out of touch with reality that they have *delusions* (false beliefs) or *hallucinations* (hearing voices or seeing things that are not really there).

Episodes of mania usually come on suddenly. Symptoms tend to get worse over a few days. These periods can last for days or even weeks. They often end suddenly and may be followed by deep depression.

Some people experience the less intense state of hypomania ("hypo" is Greek for "under" or "below"), usually between bouts of depression. This is a less severe form of mania. If you experience hypomania you'll likely feel more energetic, more active and more creative. Because hypomania is less severe, you and your doctor may not even see it as part

Symptoms of Mania

Physical:
- less need for sleep
- increased sex drive
- changes in appetite

Emotional:
- "high" or euphoric moods
- angry, irritated, or agitated moods
- mood swings

Cognitive:
- racing thoughts; thought patterns that change rapidly
- inability to pay attention; easily distracted
- poor judgement.
- greatly magnified thoughts about one's capabilities
- delusions or hallucinations

Behavioral:
- loss of self-control
- fast speech
- increased activity and sociability
- reckless, impulsive behavior

of an illness. However, the depression that often comes after hypomania may be very severe and can get in the way of work and relationships.

Studies show that most people with bipolar disorder have several periods of mania. Without treatment, episodes of mania often become more severe and more frequent over time. Bipolar disorder is more severe than major depression. If you have bipolar disorder, you're more likely to stay depressed longer, have episodes more often, have more severe symptoms, and have more delusions and hallucinations than someone with major depression.

Unlike major depression, which affects more women than men, bipolar disorder affects both men and women the same. About one in 200 people suffer from the disorder.

Dysthymic Disorder

Dysthymia is a milder, but longer-lasting form of depression. According to the National Institute of Mental Health, seven to eight million Americans—two out of three of them women—suffer from this type of mild-to-moderate depression. While it has less of an impact on daily life than an episode of major depression, the gloominess of dysthymia rarely lifts. It's like an annoying little cold that you

Symptoms of Dysthymia

Physical:
- overeating or undereating
- chronic fatigue, low energy
- lack of sexual desire

Emotional:
- feelings of depression or irritability that last for days or months without lifting
- critical of self
- low self-esteem
- feelings of hopelessness or helplessness
- brooding

Cognitive:
- difficulty concentrating
- problems making decisions

Behavioral:
- preoccupation with health; fears of major health problems when you have minor symptoms

can't get rid of. Dysthymia lasts at least two years, while major depression usually lifts within 6 to 12 months. If you have dysthymia, you probably laugh and joke once in a while. You even enjoy yourself sometimes. But most of the time you feel down. Your outlook is gloomy. You often feel irritable and frustrated. You may complain a lot. Even the smallest disruptions in life cause you problems. Others may see you as pessimistic, overly critical of yourself, or lacking motivation. Untreated, dysthymia can put you at greater risk for developing major depression. Many people with dysthymia don't even know that they have a mood disorder. They often come to believe that their feelings—always down in the dumps and unable to take pleasure from life—are simply part of their personalities; or they start to think that their lives are so bad that they *should* always be sad. They don't know why, but they've felt this way for as long as they can remember. It's only after they've been treated and the chronic depression lifts that they see how depressed they have been.

Seasonal Affective Disorder (SAD)

Most people feel good about warm, sunny days and grumpy about long periods of dreary days. However, in the past 10 years doctors have noted a more serious reaction to the seasons and to sunlight. It is called *seasonal affective disorder* (SAD). People with SAD have periods of depression and sometimes hypomania. These feelings happen at the same time each year. For most, SAD depression comes on in November or December when daylight hours are short, and stays until March or April when the days get longer. Some people with SAD have hypomania during the spring and summer months.

If you have seasonal affective disorder, the shorter winter days are likely to find you feeling depressed, sluggish, irritable, and anxious. You sleep more—often up to 12 hours a day—but wake feeling tired and sluggish. You crave carbohydrates (sugar and starch), especially in the afternoon and evening, and you may put on weight. Your internal clock may shift—during one season you may be a morning person; during another, you may be a night person.

SAD can affect anyone, even children. Although doctors aren't sure why, nearly 80 percent of people with SAD are women. It can begin at any

Symptoms of Seasonal Affective Disorder

Physical:

- fatigue, sluggishness
- need for more sleep than normal (hypersomnia)
- weight gain
- craving for carbohydrates

Emotional:

- feelings of depression during the fall and winter months
- thoughts of suicide
- feelings of elation, euphoria, and increased energy in the spring and summer months

age, but usually starts around age 20 and becomes less common between 40 and 50.

Suicide Alert

If you or someone you love has major depression, bipolar disorder, or seasonal affective disorder, suicide may be on your or their mind. Suicide attempts often follow a stressful event such as divorce, problems at work, or medical illness. Anytime you feel you or someone you love is showing any of the signs below, please talk to someone right away. You need to know that it is the depression that is causing these feelings, and that there is help.

Suicide Warning Signs

- severe hopelessness
- withdrawal from activities, friends, family
- substance abuse
- giving away possessions
- depression related to serious medical illness

Things to keep in mind about suicide:

- Treatment for your depression will help get rid of your thoughts of suicide.

- Make a contract with someone you trust (friend, counselor, health care provider) to call him or her any time you think about suicide.

- Substance abuse can cause suicidal feelings. Stopping your use of alcohol or drugs can make a big improvement in how you feel.

- Take temptations out of your way. If you have things in the house that could be used in a suicide attempt, get rid of them.

- Try making a list of positive things to think about when you're feeling really down.

- **Don't be afraid to call for help. Crisis lines are open around the clock. Check the *Resources* section on pp. 93–94 at the back of this book, or your local phone book.**

What Causes Mood Disorders?

The brain and the nervous system are complex. Medical experts don't know exactly what causes most mood disorders. Some mood disorders start in response to an event such as the loss of a loved one. Other mood disorders seem to happen for no reason. Most mental health experts agree that **heredity**, biology, and environmental factors can all play a role. In many cases, it's many factors that bring on a mood disorder.

Heredity

Some experts think that some people inherit certain personality traits that may make them more likely to develop depression. These traits include being:

- pessimistic

- brooding

- very critical of self and others

Experts haven't found one single genetic cause for mood disorders. They do think that people can inherit a higher chance of developing major depression or bipolar disorder. However, the fact that mood disorders run in your family doesn't mean you will have the condition.

Biology

Brain science is still new, but in the past several years, experts have found problems in the brain that may contribute to mood disorders. Many brain experts think that chemicals called **neurotransmitters** are involved in mood disorders. These chemicals carry nerve impulses from one nerve site (neuron) to the next. However, since there are hundreds of neurotransmitters in the brain that doctors haven't even found yet, it's probable that they haven't found all of the biochemical keys to mood disorders.

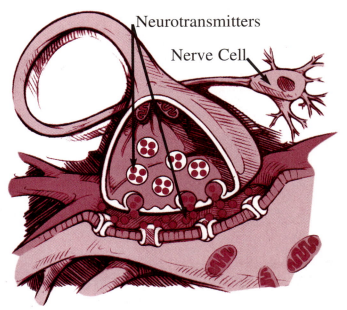

Neurotransmitters

Nerve Cell

Stress and Life Events

Major stressors such as the loss of a loved one, and even minor stressors like job dissatisfaction, can be factors in depression. It's normal to grieve after a loss. This reaction usually lasts two to six months and gets better over time without treatment. Most grief reactions do not become major depressions. However, some people have major depression along with a grief reaction.

Most mental health experts now agree that recent life event stressors such as divorce, illness, legal troubles, or grief over the loss of a loved one often come before a depressive episode. Some experts think that events from the past, such as the loss of parents, or sexual, emotional, or physical abuse in childhood, can lead to depression as an adult. One study showed that 51 percent of people suffering from major depression had lost a parent during childhood, as compared to 16 percent of people without depression. Later studies suggest that the children who have lost a parent are more likely to have depression as adults. This may be because they did not have enough support from other family members.

Other stresses that can trigger depression occur during adulthood. For instance, serious medical illnesses such as cancer, heart disease, and chronic pain can cause depression. One study found that 42 percent of those hospitalized for cancer suffered from major depression. Nearly one-third who suffered from chronic pain were depressed.

Medical Conditions

Depression can be a reaction to a serious medical problem. Some people may have pain or be unable to do certain activities because of an illness. Frustration with these limitations can sometimes lead to depression. Also, several health problems can look like or even cause mood disorders. Neurological conditions like multiple sclerosis, Parkinson's disease, and stroke can trigger depression or mania. Problems with the thyroid and Cushing's disease, an endocrine condition, have been linked with high rates of depression. People who have autoimmune problems such as rheumatoid arthritis and systemic lupus also have higher rates of depression.

Patients with depression tend to complain about many minor aches and pains, such as headache or backache. In one study, over 67 percent of people with depression, versus less than 20 percent of those without, had two or more pain symptoms that got in the way of their daily lives.

Possible Medical Causes of Mood Disorders

The following is a partial list of the many problems your health care provider must rule out before diagnosing a mood disorder:

- Addison's disease
- Cushing's disease
- premenstrual syndrome (PMS) in women
- pituitary gland disorder

(continued, next page)

- mononucleosis

- hypothyroidism

- thyroid imbalance

- estrogen deficiency in women (especially at menopause)

- ovarian failure in women

- hyperparathyroidism

- allergies

- narcolepsy

- sleep apnea

- neurological illnesses (Parkinson's disease, Alzheimer's, multiple sclerosis)

Chronic physical pain from an accident, injury, or chronic medical illness is a major stressor and often leads to secondary depression. It seems, then, that depression leads to pain, and chronic pain leads to depression.

Drugs

Alcohol, illicit drugs, and even prescription medicines can cause depression. Alcohol has been linked with depression for quite some time. However, experts don't know which of these is the cause and which is the effect. Alcohol and other drugs may offer the depressed person

Drugs Linked to Depression

- antihypertensives (used to control high blood pressure) such as reserpine, methyldopa, thiazides, spironolactone, and clonidine hydrochloride

- oral contraceptives (birth control pills)

- steroids and adrenocorticotropic hormones, anabolic steroids (used by bodybuilders to build muscle mass)

- cimetidine and ranitidine (used to treat ulcers)

- barbiturates (central nervous system depressants used to treat anxiety and insomnia, or to control seizures)

- benzodiazepines (used to treat anxiety and sleeplessness)

- beta-blockers (used to treat high blood pressure and sometimes anxiety), especially propranolol hydrochloride

- metoclopramide hydrochloride (used to treat various stomach problems)

- cocaine

- amphetamines (central nervous system stimulants used to treat attention deficit disorder, hyperactivity, and narcolepsy)

relief from feelings of depression for a short time. However, over time, the drugs themselves worsen the depression. Doctors believe that, in order to determine whether alcohol is causing depression, a person must stop drinking for three to four weeks.

Several prescription drugs have been linked with depression. Unfortunately, doctors often don't know if the drugs actually cause the depression, since doctors rarely check people for depression before they begin taking the drug. However, some of the drugs listed above may have side effects like depression.

Lack of Sunlight

Doctors think that seasonal affective disorder (SAD) has to do with the decreased sunlight available in the winter months. Sunlight plays a central role in regulating many biological processes that run on daily cycles.

Some experts theorize that SAD is linked with the pineal gland, a small reddish-gray structure near the center of the brain. Resembling a small pinecone, the pineal gland is thought to help us adjust to changes in the yearly day-night cycles. When there is less light, the pineal gland sends out more melatonin, a natural sleep-causing hormone. This hormone seems to depress both mood and mental agility. People with SAD seem to have higher levels of melatonin during their depressive periods.

Other experts believe melatonin is simply a biological marker that signals the body clock is out of sync with cues from the environment (light and dark). These experts think the various daily biological rhythms become unhinged from one another and people with SAD feel a severe jet lag.

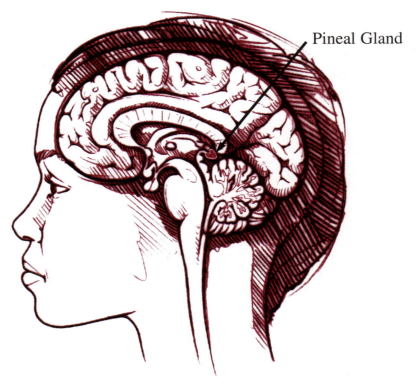

Pineal Gland

WHO'S AT RISK FOR MOOD DISORDERS?

People of all ages, races, and social or economic backgrounds can have mood disorders. No one can tell who will develop them. However, mental health experts say you're at increased risk if you have:

- had a mood disorder before

- a close relative who has had mood disorders

- personal or family history of suicide attempts

- current substance abuse

- had early childhood abuse or neglect

- had a recent stressful life event or lack of social support

- a current medical illness

- symptoms of fatigue, malaise (generally not feeling well), irritability, or sadness

Also, some groups are at more risk than others. Mental health experts say that women, children (especially adolescents), and the elderly carry a special risk for mood disorders.

During a lifetime, 20 to 25 percent of women will have a major depressive episode as compared to only 10 percent of men. Evidence suggests that more moderate depression is 10 times more common for women than for men. There may be other factors that add to the high rate of depression in women.

Hormonal factors. A woman's body is influenced by hormones such as estrogen throughout her lifetime. These changes can make her more vulnerable to depression. For instance, women with premenstrual syndrome (PMS) often feel depressed just before or during their period. Even women who undergo hysterectomies may suffer from depression due to the sudden drop-off in the body's production of estrogen.

Pregnancy is a time that causes major shifts in a woman's hormones and her moods. ***Postpartum*** depression is a catchall term for a variety of mental conditions that can start after childbirth. "Maternity blues" or "baby blues" occur in 50 to 80 percent of mothers, usually three to four days after giving birth. The new mother feels an episode of sadness, weeping, anxiety, headache, sleep disorders, or irritability. This generally lasts one to two weeks. Doctors think it's a normal response to the hormonal changes and it usually goes away without treatment. But sometimes the maternity blues signal the start of a more serious postpartum depression.

Postnatal depression is a more severe depression. About 10 percent of new mothers feel the severe hopelessness, mood swings, guilt, sleep disturbances, and sometimes irritability of postnatal depression. It usually occurs two weeks to four months after delivery. Postnatal depression usually goes away within two to eight weeks. However, about 25 to 43 percent of women who have an episode of postnatal depression still have some symptoms a year later. One-third to one-half of these mothers will have another postnatal depressive experience if they have another child.

About one in 1,000 new mothers has postpartum psychosis. This includes episodes of mild depression, paranoia, confusion, incoherence, nightmares, delusions, delirium, hallucinations, and thoughts of harming themselves or their babies.

If you or a loved one have symptoms of postpartum psychosis, please see a mental health professional right away.

Psychological factors. In our culture, women and men often learn to deal with emotions differently. While men are often taught to hide their emotions, women are generally encouraged to express how they feel. In fact, the statistics that suggest depression is more common among women may, in part, be due to the fact that women are more likely to be aware of and report their emotional problems.

Social factors. Women also face unique social issues that may help cause depression. For instance, women are more likely to be sexually abused or battered than men. Today, women often face conflicting demands as mothers, wives, and employees. They often earn far less than male co-workers. Surveys show that young women who have children and little support in raising them make up one of the highest risk groups for major depression. Young or middle-aged women who have children and who have been widowed are also at higher risk for clinical depression.

Children

According to the National Institute of Mental Health, 2 out of every 100 children under the age of 12 have some form of depressive illness. In adolescents, the chance is twice as high. Sadly, many of these children go undiagnosed and untreated.

It wasn't until the 1960s that mental health experts even thought that children could have mood disorders. Even today, many parents, teachers, and other caregivers don't think that children can have depression or bipolar disorder. Most of us want to imagine childhood as a carefree time, not a time filled with anxiety, anger, or sadness.

Mental health experts think the causes of mood disorders in children are the same as in adults. Even the symptoms—sadness, fatigue, sleep disturbances, feelings of hopelessness—are similar. However, children may show their symptoms differently, which makes spotting mood disorder problems harder. For instance, a depressed or bipolar adolescent may seem irritable, sulky, and sloppy. His or her symptoms might be mistaken for normal, rebellious teen behavior. Mood disorder symptoms may be masked in a variety of behavior problems such as disruptiveness, bed-wetting, fighting, school problems, and alcohol or drug abuse. Or the child may show his or her mood disorder symptoms as physical complaints such as headaches, stomachaches, back or neck pain.

Children often have a hard time telling others that they feel depressed. When asked what the problem is, a depressed youngster may only shrug and pout. A child who is quiet and withdrawn may be thought good, when he or she is actually depressed.

Just as there is no single cause of mood disorders in adults, doctors think many factors cause depressive or bipolar disorders in children. Often there is a strong family link. Research shows that even infants of depressed parents can become depressed.

Environment plays a role in children's depression too. The death of a loved one, divorce, adjusting to a new family situation, a physical illness or handicap, or other stresses can be linked to childhood depression. Children in families where there is sexual, physical, or emotional abuse are more at risk for depression. Depression is also common among children whose parents are highly critical and demanding and those whose parents don't spend meaningful interactive time with them.

Mood disorders in young people can result in learning problems, school failure, drug abuse and addiction, poor relationships, tendency to illness, or violent behavior. Perhaps most tragically, mood disorders can result in suicide. More than 5,000 children commit suicide every year. In fact, suicide is now the second leading cause of death among youth ages 15 to 24.

Suicide is a very real concern among children with mood disorders. It is more common among adolescents, but children as young as 5 or 6 have tried to kill themselves. Suicide attempts often follow a stressful event— the breakup of a romance, the divorce of parents, disciplinary action, problems in school, or failure to win an award, honor, or position. If your child shows any of the signs in the following list, talk with him or her *right away*. Help your child talk about what's going on.

How Can You Know If Your Child Has a Mood Disorder?

If your child has a number of the following symptoms for two weeks or more, call for professional help. The first step should be a complete medical exam to rule out any physical problems.

- Does your child have a poor self-image? Does he or she put him- or herself down or take the blame for problems that were not his or her fault?

- Has your child lost interest in activities he or she used to enjoy? Does the child appear bored and apathetic even when playing a favorite game or with a favorite toy?

- Has your child had changes in his or her sleep patterns? Does he or she resist going to bed at the normal time? Has he or she been having many nightmares? Is the child very hard to get up in the morning? Does the child seem lethargic?

- Does your child seem to have trouble paying attention? Has the teacher noted he or she isn't paying attention in class? Have you seen that he or she is easily distracted? Have the child's grades fallen?

- Is your child more irritable than usual? Do minor frustrations spark tantrums or irritations that last a long time? Has the child been unusually aggressive toward others?

- Has your child's appetite changed? Has there been a major change in his or her weight?

- Has your child shown unusual risk-taking behavior? Does he or she ignore basic safety rules? Is the child more accident-prone than usual?

- Does the child complain of unknown physical problems? Does he or she have many headaches, stomachaches, or other ailments for which no cause can be found?

- Has your child talked about death or suicide?

Suicide Red Alert

Parents, relatives, teachers, and other caregivers need to be alert for the following signs of childhood and adolescent suicide:

- increased sadness, tearfulness, moodiness, or irritability
- withdrawal from favorite activities or friends and family
- signs of drug or alcohol abuse
- changes in sleeping and/or eating habits
- sudden problems in school
- unusually great concern with death and dying
- giving away worldly goods such as favorite tapes, toys, or other possessions
- recent personal loss

The Elderly

People over the age of 65 may be at higher risk for mood disorders. According to the U.S. Department of Health and Human Services, 3 out of every 100 people age 65 and over have depression. Depression in the elderly can cause unneeded suffering, antisocial behavior, early retirement, overuse of social and medical services, unnecessary hospital and nursing home admissions, alienation from friends and family, and even death. Elderly people account for 25 percent of the suicides in the United States.

Mental health experts say there are a number of factors, in addition to the ones already talked about in this book (see **What Causes Mood Disorders?**, pp. 15–20), that make older people more susceptible to depression.

Losses. One cannot live a long life without facing many losses—death of friends and family members, loss of career or status, change in living situation, decline of physical and mental powers, loss of independence, and decrease of income, among others. For some older people, the accumulation of these losses results in depression.

Diseases of old age. Long-term or sudden illness can bring on or worsen depression. Also, elderly people are more likely to have illnesses linked with depression (See **Possible Medical Causes of Mood Disorders**, pp. 17–18). One study of aging adults showed that the most common factor in the start of depression was a serious physical illness in either themselves or their spouses.

Often clinical depression is missed or misdiagnosed because it is hidden among many physical complaints. An older person is less likely to complain of depression than of headaches, backaches, constipation, or fatigue.

Medicines. Older people use 25 percent of all prescription medicines. Most older people take several medicines per day. Many of these drugs, separately or in combination, can cause symptoms of depression and several other dangerous drug interactions. (See **Drugs Linked to Depression**, p. 19.)

If You Think You May Have a Mood Disorder

Take the quiz below. If you answer yes to several of the questions and these symptoms have lasted for at least two weeks, you need to see a health care professional for evaluation.* **If you answer yes to question 3, seek professional help right away regardless of your quiz results.**

Do You Suffer From a Mood Disorder?
Answer yes or no

1. I feel downhearted, blue, and sad . . . .❏Yes ❏No
2. I don't enjoy the things I used to do . . . .❏Yes ❏No
3. I think about or have tried suicide . . . .❏Yes ❏No
4. I feel I'm not useful or needed . . . .❏Yes ❏No
5. I have been losing or gaining weight . . . .❏Yes ❏No

(continued, next page)

* For more information about the symptoms of specific mood disorders, see **Appendix: Questions From the DSM-IV**, pp. 95–98.

6. I have trouble sleeping through the night . . . .❑Yes ❑No

7. I am restless and can't keep still . . . .❑Yes ❑No

8. My mind isn't as clear as it used to be . . . .❑Yes ❑No

9. I get tired for no reason . . . .❑Yes ❑No

10. I feel hopeless about the future . . . .❑Yes ❑No

11. I feel sad and listless during the
    fall and winter months . . . .❑Yes ❑No

12. During the fall and winter, I crave carbohydrates,
    especially in the afternoon or evening . . . .❑Yes ❑No

13. I have times when I feel more energy
    and less need for sleep . . . .❑Yes ❑No

14. Sometimes thoughts come so fast, I can hardly
    communicate them . . . .❑Yes ❑No

15. During these times of great energy, I often do
    things that may be risky to myself or others . . . . .❑Yes ❑No

SECTION II:
GETTING HELP FOR
MOOD DISORDERS

You will likely have many choices for how you wish to treat your depression. The decision is *yours*. But it's hard to choose treatment until you know exactly what you're treating. Mood disorders should be checked by health professionals, preferably those with specialized mental health training. They are *not* something you should try to self-diagnose. Three out of four people who get proper help improve greatly. Without treatment, however, your mood disorder could lead to serious problems in your daily life, like difficulties at work and at home.

This section talks about treatment options that can help and information you need to make the best choices for your treatment, including the following topics:

- understanding the mental health care system
- diagnosing mood disorders
- treatments that can help
- self-help therapy options
- professional therapy for mood disorders
- mood disorder medicines

UNDERSTANDING THE MENTAL HEALTH CARE SYSTEM

Before you decide about treatment for a mood disorder, you want to get as much information as you can. You need to know about the services and providers available to you.

If your workplace has an Employee Assistance Program (EAP) then you can get help from these trained counselors. They help with work and personal problems by giving assessment, brief counseling, and *referrals*. Their services are often free or at a low cost to employees.

On the other hand, if you don't have an EAP, you may need to find resources yourself. In this case, learning as much as you can about how the mental health care system works can help you make better choices.

Understanding Your Benefits

Health care insurance differs in the type and extent of coverage for mental health care. Before you decide on treatment, you need to know your mental health care *benefits*. Mental health care is not an exact science, and treatment approaches, such as the number of visits and the setting, can vary. This can leave you confused, which is one of the reasons why health insurers and employers have worked to manage mental health care services. This may include a limit on the number of visits to a provider, and the types of problems covered. Your health plan may also want you to get a referral from your primary care provider. Your progress may also be checked by a case manager, a person at the health plan. All of these efforts are aimed at helping you get the best and most cost-effective care for your condition.

Professionals Who Can Help

If you decide to get professional help with your depression, there are many different types of professionals who can help.

Primary Care Provider (PCP). The first step in seeking professional treatment should be a visit your usual *primary care provider*. Your PCP can give you a physical checkup to rule out other medical causes of your depression, and give referrals to mental health professionals. In some cases, your PCP may be able to diagnose and treat your depression with medicines, if that is the treatment program you choose.

Psychiatrists. These are medical doctors who specialize in the diagnosis and treatment of mental or psychiatric disorders. A psychiatrist can provide both psychotherapy and medicine.

Psychologists. These are mental health professionals who have earned a doctoral degree (Ph.D. or Psy.D.) in psychology. They have vast knowledge and training in psychology, counseling, psychotherapy, and psychological testing. They are not medical doctors, so they cannot prescribe drugs.

Social Workers. These are people who have advanced degrees (master's level or higher) in social work (M.S.W. or L.C.S.W.). They often have extensive training in counseling.

Psychiatric Nurse Specialists. These are registered nurses (R.N.'s) with a master's degree in psychiatric nursing, who specialize in treating mental or psychiatric disorders.

Counselors. People with a wide range of education, training, and experience as mental health counselors. Some may have a bachelor's degree; others more advanced degrees. Some may have special training in certain areas of mental health. Be sure to find out about the person's credentials and if he or she has the right training to deal with mood disorders. Insurance plans may or may not cover therapy with these people.

Therapists. Many different kinds of mental health professionals are sometimes called *therapists*. Since licensure requirements vary from state to state, be sure to ask about the person's training and credentials.

Marriage and Family Therapists. These master's level mental health professionals (M.F.T. or M.F.C.C.) are specially trained to deal with issues such as marriage conflicts or those between generations. Their fees may or may not be covered by insurance companies.

Your mood disorder may need a team approach, such as a mental health therapist who can do psychotherapy and a medical doctor who can give the right medicines. Mental health therapists who can do psychotherapy but who cannot prescribe drugs often have an ongoing relationship with psychiatrists or other physicians who can act as the medicating doctor.

Tips for Working with Your Health Professional(s)

Whether you work with a medical professional or a mental health professional or both, you'll get more from your relationships and ensure that your treatment works if you follow these guidelines:

- **Be honest.** Give your doctor and/or therapist accurate information, even about areas of your life that make you feel uneasy or embarrassed. Your health care providers can help you the most when they have a true picture of you and your disorder.

- **Keep all of your appointments.** Don't stop going to your doctor or therapist just because you're feeling better. Often people feel better after a few psychotherapy sessions or a few weeks after taking medicines. Stopping your appointments too soon may harm your progress and your mood disorder will likely come back. Also, some medicines must be closely watched by your doctor.

- **Ask questions.** The only dumb questions are those that don't get asked. Don't be afraid to ask your doctor or therapist if you have concerns about your diagnosis or treatment.

- **Think about a second opinion.** If you're not satisfied with your diagnosis or treatment, or if you're not comfortable with your present doctor or therapist, ask for a referral to another provider.

- **Take your medicine exactly as prescribed.** Don't stop taking your medicine or change the dose without talking with your doctor first. Suddenly stopping some drugs can cause more depression. Make sure you understand all instructions for taking the medicine. (See page 53 for questions to ask about mood disorder medicines.)

- **Let your health care provider know about side effects.** Some medicines have *side effects*. Your doctor may be able to adjust your dose or change the medicine to relieve some of the side effects.

- **Tell your doctor or therapist how the treatment is working.** Your health care provider needs to watch and adjust your treatment, depending on how well it is working. Give him or her exact and honest feedback regularly.

How Are Mood Disorders Diagnosed?

If you have not yet been diagnosed with a mood disorder, your first step should be a visit with your primary care provider. This health care professional can help diagnose and treat your mood disorder. If needed, he or she will refer you to a mental health professional.

Your provider will base his or her diagnosis on one or more of the following areas:

- your family history of general medical disorders and mental illness
- your personal medical history
- your symptoms
- a physical exam
- laboratory test results

There is no simple test that will diagnose a mood disorder. Do not accept the diagnosis of a mood disorder without first seeing your health care provider to rule out symptoms caused by other medical conditions and/or drugs.

Areas for Evaluation

Family history. Your provider may want to know if any of your close relatives have had certain medical conditions, including those that may cause or mimic mood disorders. He or she may also want to know if any family members have a history of mental illnesses such as suicide or bipolar disorder, or have been hospitalized for mental illness or neurological conditions. Include information about any relative who may have had an unexplained illness or who stayed in seclusion.

Personal medical history. Let your provider know if you now have or used to have any medical illnesses such as a heart, thyroid or neurologic disease, cancer, arthritis, or other illness. Sometimes depression can be caused by medical illness. It's also important to give information about other past depressions or mental illnesses. Include information about drugs or alcohol you use. Tell your provider about prescription and over-the-counter drugs you take and let him or her know about allergies you may have to medicines, foods, or other things.

Your symptoms. Be accurate and specific in describing your symptoms. Include both physical and mental symptoms you may be feeling. You may find it helpful to keep a journal of your symptoms so you can easily answer your provider's questions, which usually include the following:

- When did your symptoms begin?
- How often do they occur?
- Are they constant or do they come and go?
- What do they feel like?
- Have you had these symptoms in the past?
- What recent changes or stresses have you had in your life?

Physical exam and laboratory tests. Since 10 to 15 percent of depressive symptoms are caused by medical illnesses, your health care provider should do a thorough medical exam with the right laboratory tests to rule out medical conditions that may cause or mimic a mood disorder. Your doctor will likely want to do the following laboratory tests: a complete blood count, blood chemistry and electrolyte tests, thyroid tests, a serum folate level, a serum vitamin B_{12} level, and a urinalysis.

Based on the results of these tests, your provider may want to do an electroencephalogram (EEG), a painless test that measures the electrical activity of the brain. He or she may also want to do a computerized axial tomography (CAT scan), that gives a more sophisticated look at the brain.

Once your health care provider has ruled out physical causes for your symptoms, he or she may use the *Diagnostic and Statistical Manual of Mental Disorders, Fourth Edition* (popularly called the DSM-IV), to diagnose your condition. The DSM-IV is considered the best guide for diagnosing psychiatric conditions. It specifically lists the symptoms, as well as how many there must be and how often they must occur for each type of mood disorder.

The **Appendix** lists questions, adapted from the DSM-IV, to see if you *may* have a mood disorder. However, a word of caution: **Do not rely on self-diagnosis.** This data is given for informational purposes only. **Your mood disorder must be diagnosed by a health professional.** (If you disagree with your health care provider's diagnosis, ask for a referral for a second opinion.) You may want to bring the results of your self-quizzes with you when you go to your health care provider for diagnosis.

TREATMENTS
THAT CAN HELP

There are different types and different degrees of mood disorders. Likewise, you have several choices of treatment based on the specifics of your condition. Those with mild depression can usually find relief in self-help therapy groups or short-term professional counseling or therapy. People with moderate to severe depression will need more focused therapy and will likely need antidepressant medicine. Working closely with your health care providers can help you choose the right treatment for your condition.

The goal of treatment is to stop symptoms and prevent them from coming back. In choosing a treatment for your mood disorder, weigh the chances of getting better (the benefits), against the chances of possible problems with the treatment (the risks). Also think about the cost of the treatments versus the price you're paying for your mood disorder (for example, time lost from work or negative effects on personal relationships, etc.). Before choosing a treatment, ask your health care provider:

- What are the chances of getting better with this treatment?

- What are the possible risks and side effects of this treatment?

- What are the other options?

- How long will the treatment take?

- How much will this treatment cost and will it be covered by my insurance?

Stages of Treatment

Doctors and mental health professionals usually classify mood disorder treatment into three steps: acute, continuation, and maintenance.

Acute treatment: This first stage of treatment is meant to stop all the symptoms of a depressive episode. It usually lasts between 6 and 12 weeks.

Continuation treatment: The next stage of treatment is meant to keep symptoms from coming back. It usually lasts four to nine months. During this phase, those taking medicines usually keep taking them at full dosage. Those in psychotherapy continue regular sessions.

Maintenance treatment: The final stage of treatment is meant to stop the recurrence of symptoms in those with prior episodes. It may continue forever. Those taking medicines keep taking them at full dosage. Psychotherapy during this stage can also help stop recurrence.

SELF-HELP THERAPY OPTIONS

By far the most popular mental health resource is what experts call social support, and what everybody else calls friends and family. Many daily problems can be eased or even solved simply by talking about them with people who care about you.

Sometimes, though, you need more than a shoulder to cry on. You need the understanding of people who have been through similar experiences, or some practical help in dealing with depression. This is the role of self-help groups.

There are many types of self-help groups (also called mutual-help groups or support groups). Although there are differences between groups, most of them have similar roles. They help members to:

- learn more about the condition

- share feelings about the condition

- support each other's efforts to deal with the problem

In general, self-help groups rely on group members for leadership, rather than a therapist or other professional. Depending on the structure of the group, they may offer some other benefits as well, such as:

- a spiritual dimension in dealing with your depression

- a supportive atmosphere without the therapist-patient atmosphere of psychotherapy

- a new peer group to support changes you might choose to make in lifestyle or behavior

- referral to other resources for help in dealing with mood disorders

- help understanding the nature of your mood disorder and the process of dealing with it

- ways to cope and deal with your depression

- community resources to support or replace counseling/therapy

Self-help groups can range in size and structure from national organizations to local, informal groups of friends who meet regularly to talk. With so many different types of groups to choose from, it's important to choose one that offers what you need.

Where Can I Find Self-Help Groups?

There are many ways to find various self-help therapy options are available in your area.

- **Referral from your primary care provider.** Chances are that the health care professionals you see on a regular basis can suggest a number of groups in your area.

- **Telephone directory.** Many groups are listed by name in the White Pages. Some phone books have a special section on community services that lists groups by topic. In the Yellow Pages, self-help groups will be listed under topics like Mental Health or Social Services.

- **Self-help clearinghouses.** Some states, provinces, and regions have self-help clearinghouses that can refer you to groups in your area.

- **Hotlines.** National and even local organizations often have hotlines (some toll-free) that can refer you to local groups. See the **Resources** section at the end of this book for names and phone numbers of some of these groups.

- **Churches, synagogues, or temples.** Many religious organizations sponsor groups, so ask your religious leader or check with local houses of worship.

- **Newspapers.** Newspapers often have listings of group meetings.

- **Word-of-mouth.** Someone who has had similar problems with depression might be able to suggest a group.

How Do I Know Which Self-Help Group Is Right for Me?

> **Jeanne:**
>
> " Before I joined my self-help group six years ago, I wasn't functioning at all. I had been depressed for 16 years. This group helped me replace my insecure thoughts with secure ones, and gave me practical tools to overcome the "defeatist babble of the brain." I learned to congratulate myself for my efforts, not just for succeeding. Now, I've regained my spontaneity and my sense of humor. I'm working again. It really helped me to help myself. "

Self-help groups are a low-cost mental health resource available to just about everyone. But before you join a self-help group, think about what you want from the group. Use the questions below to start thinking about what's important to you in a group. The comments include some more points to think about.

1. **Is the group run by professionals (for example, therapists or physicians)?** Professionals can have both good and not-so-good

effects on a self-help group. Professionals can provide information and a link with research on mood disorders. On the other hand, some groups have found that professional leaders sometimes take over and run the group themselves, rather than letting members take the lead in helping each other.

2. **Will I "graduate" from the group eventually, or do members stay with the group forever?** The goal of many groups is to help members get along in the "outside world," without the support of the group. Others encourage members to stay with the group for support.

3. **Does the group charge a fee? If so, what does it cover?** Some possible uses of group fees are meeting costs, guest speakers, advertising, and education.

4. **What are group meetings like? Is everyone expected to take part? Are there rules, and if so, what are they?** Some groups allow people to watch, while others expect everyone to participate. Make sure you are comfortable with the group's format.

5. **What is the target population for the group? Am I a member of that population? Do I want to belong to a group for that population?** There are pros and cons to joining a group of people who are like you. You may feel more comfortable if you have a lot in common with the other group members. On the other hand, a group of similar people may lack fresh outlooks and different viewpoints.

Many types and degrees of mood disorders respond well to *psychotherapy* or a mix of medicine and psychotherapy. There are different kinds of therapy, different settings, and different kinds of therapists. Whatever the details of your therapy, you will be working with a trained professional called a *therapist*.

Note: There are two specialized therapy treatments for mood disorders that may be used in a more clinical setting as opposed to the counseling atmosphere of psychotherapy. These are *electroconvulsive therapy* and light therapy. You'll find details about these two special therapies at the end of this section.

PROFESSIONAL THERAPY FOR MOOD DISORDERS

Who Are Therapists?

A therapist is a licensed professional who has done supervised postgraduate training and passed the appropriate state or national examinations. We've looked at some of these already (see **Professionals Who Can Help**, pp. 31–32).

What Do Therapists Do?

Approaches to therapy are almost as numerous as the individuals who practice them, but they share common goals. Your therapist will:

- help you define your problem

- look at the severity of your signs and symptoms

- guide you toward the right care if more intensive help (medicine, intermediate care, or hospitalization) is needed

Psychotherapy

Studies show that psychotherapy—sessions in which the person talks about his or her feelings, thoughts, contact with others, and behaviors with a skilled mental health therapist—can be quite helpful in treating mood disorders, especially depression.

Psychotherapy usually works gradually. Many people start to feel better right away, but, for others, it may take eight to ten weeks. Psychotherapy works well for many people, especially those with mild to moderate depression (those with bipolar disorder often need a mix of medicine and psychotherapy). Over 50 percent of those with mild to moderate depression respond well to psychotherapy.*

Three forms of psychotherapy have proven particularly effective for mood disorders: *cognitive therapy*, *behavioral therapy*, and *interpersonal therapy*.

Cognitive therapy. This time-limited therapy (typically 10 to 25 weeks) is based on the concept that certain thoughts make negative feelings. Change those thoughts and the unhappy emotions will change, too. For instance, a person may lose a job and believe "I am worthless if I'm not working." The therapist would help that person see that he or she has value as a person apart from work. The person may then think "One way I contribute to the world is through work, but I'm also a good parent/partner/community member. I'm just as worthwhile even though I'm not working right now." The therapist helps the person notice and change problematic thoughts and beliefs and build a better self-image based on reality.

Behavioral therapy. While cognitive therapy focuses on changing a person's thoughts, behavioral therapy focuses on changing observable behaviors. For instance, people who are depressed often do few enjoyable things. A behavioral therapist may help someone identify and spend time doing more pleasant activities. As a result, the person's mood improves. Also, a behavioral therapist might teach relaxation techniques to help the person come to a state of deep relaxation. (See **Learn Relaxation Techniques**, p. 83, for more information on relaxation techniques.) Another technique used by behavioral therapists is desensitization, in which the person is exposed little by little over time to situations, objects, or places that cause anxiety or other disturbing feelings. Behavioral therapists often use positive reinforcement/ extinction, in which desired behaviors are encouraged and negative behaviors are discouraged and finally eliminated. Some therapists use a mix of cognitive and behavioral therapies to treat mood disorders.

Interpersonal therapy. This type of therapy is also time-limited (typically about 12 sessions). It focuses on how relationships with family,

* U.S. Department of Health and Human Service's Agency for Health Care Policy and Research

44

friends, co-workers, and others impact how we feel about ourselves and our lives. Interpersonal therapists help resolve conflicts about past and present relationships and work to improve the person's self-image and communication skills.

If you prefer a specific type of therapy, you'll need to find a therapist who offers that therapy. Also, be sure to check with your health insurance representative to see what coverage, if any, your policy has for that therapy. Many policies provide full or partial coverage for some types of therapies (or therapists), but not for others.

Other Therapy Considerations

When you're choosing therapy, there are several other things to think about: who will be involved in the therapy, and where will the therapy take place?

Therapy can be in a one-to-one setting with the client and the therapist (*individual therapy*). It may involve your partner and/or other family members (*family therapy*). Or it may be a therapist-led group working out its problems together (*group therapy*). How you answer the question "who will be involved in therapy?" depends on the nature of the problems you need to address, the willingness of others to take part in therapy, and the availability of different therapy settings in your area.

Where will your therapy take place? If you are seeing a therapist in private practice, often the sessions will take place in his or her office, but there are other options as well. Community mental health centers or clinics sometimes offer therapy at lower rates than those charged by therapists in private practice. Family therapy is sometimes held in the client's home, where the therapist can deal with the family in its normal setting. Home therapy is also an option for the elderly, people receiving home health care, or for those with no transportation.

While it's important to know the general differences in therapies, choosing a certain type of therapy may not be a crucial decision for you. Many therapists draw techniques from more than one type of therapy, based on the needs of the patient. Also, some studies have shown that successful therapy depends more on the relationship between the client and the therapist than on the specific type of therapy used.

Note: Beware of fads. The field of psychotherapy is always changing. There are many types of therapy that can claim success with some patients. Yet this diversity means that the field is also open to fads. Be careful of therapies that rely on testimonials from patients rather than the support of scientists. If you have doubts about a certain type of therapy or a certain clinic or provider, call your state or local Department of Mental Health, or check with your doctor, EAP, or managed care professional.

How to Find the Best Therapist for You

You wouldn't buy a major appliance without shopping around and doing a little research. It's very important that you find the right therapist to help you with your mood disorder. After all, some types of mood disorders need long-term management. You need health care professionals you can trust and with whom you can work over time. You need someone with whom you can freely discuss your treatment, and talk about your concerns—someone who can answer your questions and give you clear explanations and instructions.

If you are a member of a managed care organization, you may feel your freedom to choose your health care providers is limited. However, this is not always true. Your freedom starts when you choose your health care coverage. If you have a choice between different plans, research the plans and the providers working with the plans before you enroll. Perhaps you don't have a choice of plans. However, you can choose your primary care provider and specialists you might see within that plan. Talk with possible PCPs and potential mental health specialists about your mood disorder and their approach.

You may already have a mental health therapist whom you like and trust. If not, here are a few ideas to help you find the providers that are right for you:

- **Ask for referrals.** Rely on suggestions from people you know and trust. Ask your friends and family about their experiences with doctors and therapists in your area. If you know a doctor or nurse personally, ask them for names of therapists whom they trust. You can also call one of the agencies listed in the **Resources** section on pp. 93–94 at the back of this book for a list of specialists dealing with mood disorders in your area.

- **Check out qualifications.** It's pretty easy to get some basic information on doctors, such as where he or she went to medical school (it should be fully accredited) and did postgraduate training or residency (large, well-known hospitals usually have excellent postgraduate programs). Ask your local librarian for medical directories, including the *Directory of Medical Specialists*.

It can be harder checking out a non-medical therapist's qualifications. There are many schools of psychological training. In some states, mental health therapists must be state-licensed or certified to practice. This license means that the therapist has met the minimum qualifications.

- **Have a first interview.** Some doctors and therapists will take a few minutes to talk with you on the phone. Others will want you to come in for a visit. Ask about the person's experience in treating mood disorders, his or her approach, treatment options, and anything else that may concern you. Look for these qualities:

  ➤ **Experience.** Treating some types of mood disorder requires specialized expertise. Look for professionals who have training, experience, and a good track record in treating mood disorders like yours.

  ➤ **Good communication skills.** Did this person talk clearly with you? Did he or she use everyday words or medical lingo? Did you have his or her complete attention? Is the person a good listener? Were you able to ask all your questions? Did he or she take time to talk with you or did you feel rushed?

  ➤ **Empathetic.** It's important that you feel that your therapist (and any other health care professional you see) understands and cares about you. Do you feel the person is interested in you and is concerned about your health? Does the person seem to understand what you're saying?

Finding the Right Therapist

The following checklists can help you organize your thinking. By completing this worksheet, you should be on your way to finding a therapist who is right for you. Keep in mind that you may have to meet with a few before you find the right one.

Type of therapist
Do you prefer a therapist with a certain type of training? (Remember to check and see what your insurance covers.)

- ❏ Psychiatrist
- ❏ Clinical social worker
- ❏ Marriage/family therapist
- ❏ Psychologist
- ❏ Psychiatric nurse specialist
- ❏ Counselor
- ❏ No specific preference

Personal issues
Do you prefer certain personal characteristics in a therapist?

- ❏ Certain gender
- ❏ Certain age group
- ❏ Personality traits
- _____

Referrals
Check below all your possible sources for referrals.

- ❏ Friends/family
- ❏ EAP/benefits counselor
- ❏ Primary care provider
- ❏ Hospital or medical center
- ❏ Other _____
- ❏ Community mental health center
- ❏ Managed care professional
- ❏ Priest, minister, or rabbi
- ❏ Public library

Credentials
When you meet with a therapist, be sure to ask about his or her credentials, including:

- ❏ Degrees earned
- ❏ State licensure
- ❏ Certification earned
- ❏ Supervision and experience

Therapy setting
Do you prefer a certain therapy setting?

- ❏ Private office
- ❏ Hospital outpatient clinic
- ❏ Home
- ❏ Community mental health clinic
- ❏ Group therapy
- ❏ Other: _____

Insurance
If health insurance covers mental health treatment, check your coverage for the following:

- ❏ Limit on the number of visits?
- ❏ Limit on the amount spent (yearly, lifetime)?
- ❏ Does policy cover the type of therapist I want to see?
- ❏ Does policy cover the type of therapy I want?

➤ **Comfortable personality.** The chemistry between your personality and the therapist's must work. Do you feel comfortable with this person? If gender or age are important, does this person fit what you're looking for? Is this person friendly and respectful? Listen to your gut reactions.

Electroconvulsive Therapy

For people with severe depression who don't respond to medicines, psychotherapy, or combination therapy, *electroconvulsive therapy (ECT)* can be used to end symptoms. Modern ECT is the best treatment for severe depression. In fact, more than 80 percent of severely depressed people respond to ECT. It is a painless, safe, and effective treatment for severe depression and life-threatening mania.

ECT is done in a hospital with a psychiatrist, an anesthesiologist, and nursing staff. The person is given a short-acting anesthetic, oxygen, and a temporary muscle paralyzer. Electrodes attached to the head send a very small electric current into the brain for 25 to 60 seconds. An electroencephalogram (EEG) watches the brain activity while an electrocardiogram (EKG) watches heart rhythm. After several minutes, the person wakes from the anesthesia with no memory of the event. Some people have a brief period of confusion, headache, or muscle stiffness, but these symptoms usually pass within 30 to 60 minutes.

ECT is usually given every other day for six to eight treatments. Some people need as few as three or four treatments; others may need anywhere from 12 to 30. To prevent relapse, some people need antidepressant drugs or lithium, or single ECT treatments every four to six weeks.

Light Therapy

Light therapy has been shown to work well for people with SAD. This therapy uses special light boxes that shine full-spectrum light up to 20 times brighter than normal indoor lighting. The person sits or stands a few feet away from the light box for a certain amount of time, often first thing in the morning when the eye's retina is most sensitive to light. How much light is needed varies with the person. Some people need as little as 15 minutes a day with the light box; others need up to 2 hours.

While light therapy sounds easy, it is *not* something you can do yourself. Too much light can be too stimulating, making you feel anxious and hypomanic. It's important to work with a clinician to be sure that you're getting the right amount of light for the right length of time.

MOOD DISORDER MEDICINES

Medicines play a big role in the treatment of mood disorders. Often, medicine is used along with psychotherapy, in what is called combined treatment. Medicines are often used when the doctor or therapist thinks that biology plays a big part in the mood disorder. The therapist or doctor may also suggest medications if your symptoms are very disruptive to your life or to therapy. The U.S. Department of Health and Human Services says you should think about medicine as an option if your symptoms have been helped by medicine in the past, or if your symptoms are:

- severe

- chronic

- recurrent (two or more past episodes)

- accompanied by hallucinations or delusions

- like those of others in your family

- not responsive to psychotherapy alone

If you think drug treatment might help you, and your doctor or therapist has not mentioned it, bring it up. Your therapist should be able to give a medication referral to a psychiatrist or other physician.

Medical consultation visits are quite different from psychotherapy sessions. The visits are often short—15 to 30 minutes—and usually take place every two to four weeks (psychotherapy is often weekly). The purpose is to see how well the medicine is working.

The first medical consultation will likely take an hour or longer. The doctor may or may not prescribe medicine after the first visit. He or she should ask about your current symptoms and any personal or family history with mental illness. The doctor will want to know about your history, including your childhood, school, work, relationships, and other current stressors. He or she will want to know your medical history and your past use of drugs and alcohol. Psychiatrists often also test brain functions such as memory, concentration, and the ability to do simple math. If you haven't already had a thorough medical exam, including the right laboratory tests, be sure the doctor gives one to rule out medical conditions that may be causing your condition. Also let the doctor know about any other drugs you're taking to prevent harmful drug interactions.

There are many different types of antidepressant medicines. There is no lab test that can determine which type you need. Just because you have a certain mood disorder doesn't mean a certain medicine will work for you. Two people can have the same diagnosis, but have very different reactions to the same medicine. Finding the right medicine and the right dose often takes trial and error. Have patience. It may take weeks or months before some medicines work.

When prescribing medicines, your doctor must tailor the treatment to make sure you get the most benefit with the least risk. Together, you and your health care provider should think about:

- **Possible side effects.** Some drugs have minor side effects such as drowsiness or sleeplessness, stomach upset or weight gain. Others may have more serious side effects such as heart rhythm disturbances.

- **Your past response or unresponsiveness to certain drugs.**

- **Other drugs you may be taking and their possible drug interactions.**

- **Any other medical or mental illnesses you may have.** Some medical problems make taking certain types of drugs dangerous. For instance, if you have heart disease, you shouldn't take drugs that cause heart rhythm disturbances.

- **Your age.** As your body ages, it handles drugs differently, making drug overdoses more likely. Older people often need lower doses of medicines and need doses to be increased more slowly. Also, an older person is likely to have other medical conditions that can make treatment with drugs harder.

Before taking mood disorder medicines, be sure you understand the pros and cons, what to expect, and what to watch for. Ask your health care provider or pharmacist these questions:

1. What is the name of the medicine (both generic and brand names)?

2. When and how often should I take it?

3. What side effects can I expect? How can I reduce side effects?

4. Are there foods I should avoid while taking it?

5. Can I drink alcohol while taking it?

6. Can I take it with other drugs? What about over-the-counter drugs?

7. What should I do if I forget to take a dose?

8. How long will I have to take this drug?

9. How will I know if the medicine is working?

10. How much does it cost? Is there a generic version?

Getting the Most From Your Medicines

- Take all medicines exactly as prescribed.

- If you feel drowsy or less alert after taking your medicine, change your activities or ask your doctor if you can take the medicine at night.

- Never share your medicine. Your prescription may have a bad effect on someone else.

- Store medicines in a cool, dry place (not the bathroom).

- Keep all medicines out of the reach of children and pets.

- Order enough medicine so you won't run out during holidays or out-of-town trips.

(continued, next page)

- If you are pregnant or planning on getting pregnant, talk with your doctor. Some medicines can have a bad effect on a growing fetus.
- Don't use any medicines, including over-the-counter drugs, without talking with your doctor or pharmacist.
- Keep medicines in their original containers. Don't mix medicines in the same container.
- Set up a reminder system (keeping medicines in sight, weekly pill containers, setting alarm clocks, etc.) to help you remember to take your medicine at the right time.
- Watch for side effects and report them to your doctor right away.
- Be sure to tell any doctor or dentist about all of the medicines you're taking.

How Do Mood Disorder Medicines Work?

Depression is treated with *antidepressants*, a class of drugs that increase the amount of the brain chemicals (neurotransmitters) *norepinephrine* and *serotonin*. The mania of bipolar disorder is often controlled with lithium, a drug that helps stop the highs and lows of mania/depression episodes. Sometimes a mix of drugs may be used.

To understand how antidepressants work, it's helpful to look at how the brain communicates. Information is sent from one part of the brain to another by chemicals called neurotransmitters. An electrical signal starts in a nerve cell (*neuron*). This signal travels along the cell until it reaches a tiny gap, called a *synapse*, between that cell and the next. For the signal to be able to get across this gap, a chemical reaction happens. The neurotransmitters move into the gap and float over to the next cell where they attach at special locations called *receptor sites*. When enough of the receptor site is filled with the neurotransmitter, another electrical signal is started and the message moves along this second cell to repeat the process.

Antidepressant medicines slow a neuron function called *re-uptake*. After a neuron releases the chemical neurotransmitter, it reabsorbs

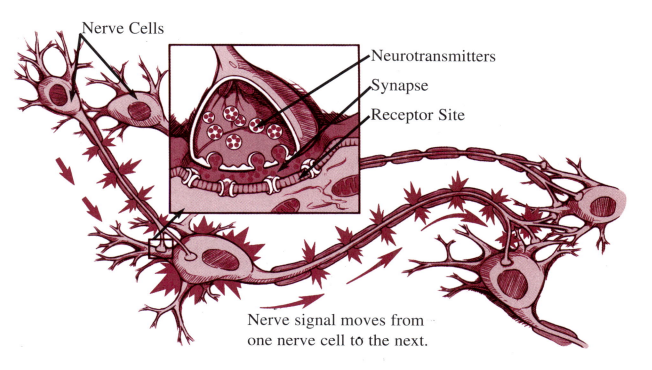

Nerve Cells

Neurotransmitters

Synapse

Receptor Site

Nerve signal moves from one nerve cell to the next.

before it is able to get to the receptor site on the next cell. Slowing re-uptake lets the neurotransmitters stay in the gap between the cells longer. This increases the signal across the gap.

There are three basic types of antidepressant medicines: **tricyclics or heterocyclics; selective serotonin re-uptake inhibitors;** and **monoamine oxidase inhibitors (MAOIs).**

Tricyclic and Heterocyclic Antidepressants

Although tricyclic antidepressants (TCAs) and heterocyclic antidepressants (HCAs) are slightly different chemically, both types of drugs increase the concentration of the brain chemicals norepinephrine and serotonin. Some increase the amount of these chemicals in the gap between nerve cells. Others block their re-uptake. (See **Drugs Commonly Used for Mood Disorders**, p. 9 , for a list of commonly used drugs.)

The good news is that TCAs and HCAs are *not* addictive. They will not intoxicate, stimulate, or make you "high" in any way. However, like other drugs, TCAs and HCAs do have side effects.

One of the most annoying side effects of TCAs and HCAs is

Possible Side Effects of Tricyclic and Heterocyclic Antidepressants

- sedation (feeling slower and more tired than usual)
- dry mouth or eyes
- strange taste in the mouth
- blurred vision, sensitivity to light
- constipation
- trouble urinating
- lightheadedness or dizziness when standing up (orthostatic hypotension)
- weight gain
- erection or ejaculation difficulties

The Following Side Effects Are Usually Shorter and Go Away As the Body Gets Used to the Medicine:

- restlessness, feeling anxious
- trembling
- increased sweating
- sleep problems, including trouble falling asleep
- trouble paying attention

sleepiness. Most people take the drugs at bedtime but sometimes the grogginess is still felt the next day. Other common side effects include dry mouth, blurred vision, constipation, and urinary retention. Fortunately, these side effects are usually more annoying than dangerous.

Side effects from these antidepressant drugs may be so bothersome that you may want to stop taking the drug within a few days. Don't do it! It takes several weeks for the drug to take effect, and, by that time, the side effects usually go away or get easier to handle.

For Best Results When Taking Tricyclic or Heterocyclic Antidepressants:

- **Be sure to have a thorough medical exam to rule out health problems like glaucoma or heart disease, which can make taking TCAs/HCAs dangerous.** Anyone who is middle-aged or older should have an electrocardiogram (EKG) to check on heart health. If you have a history of heart disease, be sure to talk to your internist or cardiologist before taking any TCA or HCA medicine

- **Take only as much of the medicine as prescribed by the doctor.** You can overdose on tricyclic antidepressants. This is the leading cause of drug-related death in the United States.

- **Follow your doctor's recommended schedule for increasing your dosage.** Your doctor will likely begin you on a low dose of TCA/HCA and then increase the dosage every few days until the right levels are reached.

- **Don't suddenly stop taking the medicine.** Stopping these drugs abruptly can cause sleeplessness, nightmares, nausea, and flu-like symptoms. When you're ready to stop taking the medicine, your doctor should give you a schedule for tapering off.

- **If you have episodes of mania, ask your doctor to prescribe a different medicine.** TCAs/HCAs can bring on mania.

- **If you're 60 years or older, talk with your doctor about prescribing lower doses for your safety and comfort.**

- **Women who are pregnant or plan on getting pregnant should talk to their doctors.** Doctors are cautious about prescribing tricyclic and heterocyclic antidepressants (as with all medicines) during pregnancy or to nursing mothers. But sometimes these medications are prescribed to women with moderate to severe depression during pregnancy or while nursing.

- **Don't drink alcohol when taking TCAs/HCAs.** These drugs magnify the depressive effects of alcohol and other sedatives.

- **Cut back on caffeine while taking TCAs/HCAs.** Drinking coffee or caffeinated beverages can make you feel more jittery than usual while you are taking these medicines.

- **Be extra careful when driving or operating machinery.** TCAs/HCAs may cause the reflexes to be less sharp at first, although these side effects decrease over time.

- **Stand up slowly.** TCAs/HCAs can cause dizziness when changing positions.

- **Use artificial saliva to counteract the dry mouth caused by TCAs/ HCAs.** Using artificial saliva, found in pharmacies, or chewing on sugarless gum or sugarless hard candies can help. Also, lack of saliva promotes tooth decay, so floss and brush regularly.

- **Eat plenty of fresh fruits, vegetables, and whole grains.** These high-fiber foods will help prevent constipation.

- **Drink plenty of water.** It will make you feel less dry and will prevent constipation.

- **Tell your doctor if you wear soft contacts.** The decreased tear production common with TCAs/HCAs can cause the buildup of a thick mucus on the lens and cause an itchy, gritty feeling. The doctor may be able to prescribe a different medication, decrease the dosage, or prescribe artificial tears.

Selective Serotonin Re-Uptake Inhibitors

The newest class of antidepressants is selective serotonin re-uptake inhibitors or SSRIs. These drugs increase the levels of a specific neurotransmitter, serotonin, in the brain. SSRI medicines seem to be very helpful in treating chronic depression and they tend to have fewer side effects than tricyclics or MAOI medicines (see page 5).

SSRIs have fewer of the side effects most common with antidepressants (dry mouth, constipation, dizziness, and blurred vision). They cause little sedation. In fact, many people on SSRI medicines claim they don't feel like they're taking medicine at all. One reason these drugs are now so popular is that they don't increase appetite or cause weight gain. In fact, many people have less appetite and less carbohydrate craving while on these drugs. Also, SSRIs can be prescribed for people at risk for suicide, because they are not likely to cause death, even with an overdose.

While SSRIs have fewer side effects, they may cause agitation, anxiety, and sleeplessness in some people. Other people taking SSRIs may have headaches, nausea, and diarrhea. For many people, SSRI side effects go away after two to three weeks of taking the drug.

For Best Results When Taking
Selective Serotonin Re-Uptake Inhibitors:

- **Have patience.** It may take as long as four to six weeks for the drugs to take effect.

- **Take the drug in the morning if you're bothered by sleeplessness.** Or talk with your doctor about prescribing a sleep medicine along with the SSRI.

- **If you have an episode of hypomania (a period of mild mania), stop taking the drug and call your doctor or therapist right away.**

Possible Side Effects of SSRI Medications

- sleeplessness
- nervousness/agitation
- nausea
- diarrhea
- tremor

Less Common Side Effects

- drowsiness
- yawning
- increased sweating
- rashes
- delayed orgasm or trouble having orgasm

Monoamine Oxidase Inhibitors

Monoamine oxidase inhibitors (MAOIs) may work well for those who find tricyclic or heterocyclic antidepressants don't work, who can't handle those drugs' side effects, or who can't take them for other health reasons. MAO is an enzyme that breaks down neurotransmitters. If there is too much MAO in the brain, signals have a hard time getting from one neuron to the next. By decreasing this enzyme, MAOIs increase the amount of neurotransmitters that carry the signals.

MAOIs can be used for major depression and some forms of anxiety disorders. The drugs seem to work very well for people who have chronic depression. MAOIs are not addictive and do not make you euphoric or "high." They also have much milder side effects (dry mouth and eyes, blurred vision, trouble urinating) than tricyclics.

The biggest drawback with MAOIs is their potential for dangerous interactions with common foods and other drugs. In the so-called "cheese reaction," the drugs interact with foods rich in the amino acid tyramine, and with other drugs, to cause a dangerous rise in blood pressure and heart rate. If untreated, this can cause a heart attack or stroke.

If you strictly avoid the offending foods and drugs, MAOIs can be taken quite safely. Most of the foods that need to be avoided entirely are unusual foods, such as chicken livers, herring, and fava beans.

MAOIs can also cause dangerously low blood pressure (hypotension), especially early in treatment. They can also cause some people mid- to late-afternoon drowsiness, weight gain, trouble having an orgasm, sleep problems (sleeplessness or drowsiness), and swelling in the ankles and fingers. Like tricyclic antidepressants, they may cause a person with bipolar disorder to swing from depression to mania.

Foods to Avoid While Taking Monoamine Oxidase Inhibitors

Avoid all high-protein foods that are aged, fermented, pickled, smoked, or contaminated with bacteria. Some of these foods can be eaten in very small amounts. Ask your doctor or pharmacist.

cheeses (all but American, cream cheese, cottage cheese, and farmer's cheese)

yogurt

fava bean pods, Chinese pea pods, Italian beans, lima beans (Green beans are OK.)

fermented sausages (salami, pepperoni, bologna, summer sausage)

pastrami, corned beef

salted or smoked fish

liver

spam or canned ham

sauerkraut

caviar, snails

pickles

pickled fish

yeast extracts (e.g. Brewer's yeast. Baked products with yeast are OK.)

avocado

figs

bananas

chianti, champagne, imported beers, nonalcoholic beer, whiskey, and other distilled spirits

chocolate

soups (canned and instant soup powders)

caffeinated beverages (coffee, tea, cola, cocoa)

soy sauce

Drugs to Avoid While Taking Monoamine Oxidase Inhibitors

While taking MAOIs, don't take any drug, particularly those listed below, without talking with your doctor or pharmacist.

cold medicines

nasal decongestants, nose drops

most sinus, allergy, hay fever, and asthma medicines

local anesthetics that contain epinephrine

meperidine (Demerol)

fluoxetine (Prozac)

clomipramine (Anafranil)

cocaine, amphetamines

For Best Results When Taking Monoamine Oxidase Inhibitor Medication:

- **Follow your food plan carefully.** Ask your doctor for a complete list of foods to avoid or limit.

- **Don't take other drugs, even over-the-counter drugs, without your doctor's OK.** Drugs such as cocaine, amphetamines, and decongestants can cause a hypertensive crisis.

- **Take your medicine with meals to help decrease low blood pressure side effects.**

- **Avoid taking MAOI medicine at bedtime.** Especially early in treatment, the drugs can overstimulate your system, causing increased sweating, anxiety, jitteriness, and headaches.

- **Take divided doses throughout the day to lessen the effects of low blood pressure.**

- **Have patience.** It will take one to four weeks for the drugs to have an effect.

- **Taper off slowly.** Follow your doctor's schedule to go off the drug to avoid withdrawal symptoms.

- **When switching from fluoxetine (Prozac) to an MAOI, give yourself four to five weeks off of the first drug before taking the other.** Serious toxic reactions have occurred when fluoxetine and MAOIs are mixed.

- **Learn how to take your own blood pressure.** Home blood pressure monitors can be bought at drug stores, medical-supply houses, or through medical self-care catalogs. Take your blood pressure whenever you have a headache or other symptom to see if you're starting a hypertensive crisis.

- **Be alert for and react to hypertensive symptoms: headache at the back of the neck, stiff neck, malaise, pounding heart, vision problems, nausea and vomiting, or sudden collapse.** If you feel any of these symptoms, stop taking the MAOI medicine and go right to the doctor's office or emergency room. (People who have frequent headaches should probably take another drug, since their headaches can be confused with hypertensive-related headaches.)

- **Ask your doctor about carrying the medicine nifedipine (Procardia, Adalat) with you to bring up your blood pressure in an emergency.** If you start symptoms of low blood pressure, place a capsule under your tongue and go to the nearest emergency room.

- **Wear a medical alert bracelet or carry a medical alert card in your wallet to alert medical personnel that you take MAOIs.**

- **Tell any doctor or dentist you're seeing that you take MAOIs.** If you need surgery, allow a week or more off the drug before the operation. Ask your dentist to give local anesthetic without epinephrine.

- **Don't mix alcohol and other depressants with MAOIs.** These drugs intensify the effects of alcohol and other depressant drugs.

- **Get up slowly.** MAOIs can cause you to feel dizzy and lightheaded if you get up from lying or sitting too quickly.

Venlafaxine (Effexor)

This is a new antidepressant that has a unique chemical structure and isn't a TCA/HCA antidepressant, an SSRI, or an MAOI. Venlafaxine slows the re-uptake of both serotonin and norepinephrine, but with fewer of the side effects most often linked with antidepressants (dry mouth, constipation, blurred vision, etc.). The most common side effect seems to be nausea. However, in most people, the nausea is gone within one to three weeks of taking the drug. Other side effects may include headache, sleepiness, sleeplessness, dizziness, nervousness, and abnormal ejaculation. At higher doses, some people have higher blood pressure, heart rate, and blood cholesterol. However, side effects are usually mild, and early studies show that some people may be able to handle venlafaxine better than other types of antidepressant medicine.

Possible Side Effects of Venlafaxine

Common Effects	Less Common Effects
• nausea	• chills
• headache	• chest pain
• sleepiness	• increased blood pressure
• dry mouth	• increased heart rate
• dizziness	• blurred vision
• sleeplessness	• rash
• nervousness	• itching
• weakness	• vomiting
• abnormal ejaculation or orgasm	• gas
• impotence	• anxiety
• constipation	• tremor
	• decreased sex drive
	• frequent urination

Nefazodone (Serzone)

Another new antidepressant is nefazodone. This drug acts much like an SSRI medicine, but is chemically unlike SSRIs. Like venlafaxine, nefazodone's side effects (dry mouth, blurred vision, constipation, etc.) are much more mild than with other types of antidepressants. The most common side effects with this new drug seems to be constipation and lightheadedness.

Unlike TCA/HCA antidepressants, SSRIs, and MAOIs, nefazodone does *not* interfere with REM sleep or "dream sleep." The drug actually improves sleep and decreases the number of times people wake up during the night.

Lithium

Lithium prevents the recurrence of mania and depression. For many people with bipolar disorder, lithium has meant the difference between lives of chaos and lives of stability. Mental health experts estimate between 60 and 80 percent of people with bipolar disorder can be helped with the drug.

While many studies have shown that lithium works well in treating mania and depression, doctors aren't really sure how it works. Some think it affects a complex biological "second messenger" system inside cells. This system passes on and amplifies signals from neurotransmitters, hormones, and other molecules. Experts think this system may work too hard in people with bipolar disorder. It seems that lithium may help slow it down.

Lithium is nonaddictive and nonsedating. At the right levels, it can be quite safe. However, effective levels are often very close to toxic levels. Severe lithium intoxication can lead to seizures, confusion, coma, and even death. That's why it is *very* important to work closely with your doctor to find and keep the right levels of lithium for you. Unfortunately, each person metabolizes and eliminates the drug differently, so it may take a little trial and error before the best levels are reached.

Lithium has side effects. Early in treatment, the drug may cause nausea, vomiting, diarrhea, fine tremors of the hands, thirst, frequent urination, fatigue, and muscle weakness. These side effects often go away within several days. However, some people keep having hand tremors and severe thirst and urination while taking the drug. Some, especially women, have urinary incontinence. Also, some people gain weight or develop an underactive thyroid (hypothyroidism) and enlarged thyroid gland (goiter) while taking the drug.

Lithium doesn't work for everyone. Some people don't like the flattening effect the drug has on moods. Others feel the side effects are too unpleasant. And still others find lithium doesn't work or only partially works. Lithium may not work for those with relatives with bipolar disorder who didn't respond to lithium, those with kidney disease, and those who have four or more manic-depressive episodes per year. If lithium doesn't work for you, your doctor may suggest other drugs or a mixture of drugs like lithium and tranquilizers.

For Best Results When Taking Lithium:

- **Take exactly the dose your doctor tells you to take.** Toxic levels are close to effective levels. Don't increase your dosage without talking to your doctor.

- **Take on schedule.** Lithium quickly leaves the body, which means your level of lithium can quickly drop below effective levels if you skip one or more doses. Dropping below an effective level may cause rapid changes in mood, including mania and depression.

- **Watch for signs of toxicity: loss of appetite, vomiting, diarrhea, fatigue, weakness, unsteadiness, slurred speech, muscle twitching, and severe shakiness.** See your doctor right away if you have any of these symptoms.

- **Have your lithium blood levels checked regularly.** At first, your dosages may be changed every three to seven days until an effective and stable blood level is reached. After that, you may check your blood level every one to three months.

- **Be sure your doctor tests your kidney function before prescribing lithium and at regular intervals thereafter.** Lithium leaves the body almost entirely through the kidneys. If the kidneys don't work, the drug stays in the body and can build to toxic levels.

- **Talk with your doctor if you're on a salt-free diet or are taking diuretics (water pills).** The less sodium in the body, the less lithium leaves the body and toxic levels can build up.

- **Cut down or eliminate alcohol.** One or two drinks may do no harm while taking lithium. However, alcohol can interact with lithium causing increased sedation, confusion, and intoxication.

- **Don't take other drugs without your doctor's approval.** Drugs such as tetracycline, erythromycin, Flagyl, ibuprofen (Advil, Nuprin, Motrin) and other nonsteroidal anti-inflammatory medications, and mefenamic acid (Ponstel) can increase your lithium blood levels and increase the risk of toxicity. If you must take these drugs, have your lithium blood levels checked often.

- **Don't take lithium if you're pregnant or you're planning on getting pregnant, as the drug can harm the fetus.** If you get pregnant while on the drug, tell your doctor right away so he or she can take you off the drug or greatly lower the dosage. Don't breast-feed while taking lithium.

Possible Side Effects of Lithium

- stomach or intestinal upset
- hand tremors
- thirst and frequent urination
- fatigue
- muscle weakness
- feelings of being dazed
- weight gain
- underactive thyroid (along with tiredness, slow reactions or thinking, feeling cold, dry puffy skin, hair loss, muscle aches, menstrual changes, and weight gain)
- strange metallic taste in the mouth

Drugs Commonly Used for Mood Disorders

Tricyclic Antidepressants

Amitriptyline (Elavil, Endep)

Clomipramine (Anafranil)

Desipramine (Norpramin, Pertofrane)

Doxepin (Adapin, Sinequan)

Imipramine (Janimine, Tofranil)

Nortriptyline (Aventyl, Pamelor)

Protriptyline (Vivactil)

Trimipramine (Surmontil)

Heterocyclic Antidepressants

Amoxapine (Asendin)

Bupropion (Wellbutrin)

Maprotiline (Ludiomil)

Trazodone (Desyrel)

Selective Serotonin Re-Uptake Inhibitors

Fluoxetine (Prozac)

Paroxetine (Paxil)

Sertraline (Zoloft)

Monoamine Oxidase Inhibitors

Isocarboxazid (Marplan)

Phenelzine (Nardil)

Tranylcypromine (Parnate)

Venlafazine (Effexor)

Nefazadone (Serzone)

Lithium

Weekly Activity Record

The U.S. Department of Health and Human Services suggests making a chart to keep track of your medicines, side effects, how you feel, and your activities. Keeping a chart like this and sharing it with your health care provider can make your treatment work better. You can cut out and copy this chart to get you started.

Day of the Week	Medicines I took Name of medicine(s) I am taking and when.	Side effects How the medicine made me feel.	Symptoms How I feel on a scale of 0-5 Bad Good 0————5	Activities Include plans and "homework" for therapy	Appointment Schedule
Sample: Monday May 15	One pill at 8 a.m. and one at 8 p.m.	Dry mouth.	3—I feel better about things today.	Went to the grocery store. Made a list of good things about my life.	Dr. Smith 3:00 p.m.
Sunday					
Monday					
Tuesday					
Wednesday					
Thursday					
Friday					
Saturday					

	Medicines I took	Side effects	Symptoms	Activities	Appointment schedule
Sunday					
Monday					
Tuesday					
Wednesday					
Thursday					
Friday					
Saturday					

Hospital Care: A Special Case

In most cases, mood disorders are treated in your doctor's or therapist's office or clinic while you go about living the rest of your life as usual. However, sometimes severe mood disorders need hospital care. In some cases, hospital care is needed to treat other medical conditions that could affect your treatment. Or your mood disorder may be severe enough that you need hospital care to adjust to your medicine. Also, if you are at great risk for suicide, hospital care may be needed until your treatments begin to work.

SECTION III: SELF-CARE STRATEGIES TO RELIEVE YOUR DEPRESSION

No matter what kind of treatment you choose for your mood disorder, there are many things you can do for yourself to relieve your depression. This section gives you suggestions on how to:

- exercise

- eat a healthy diet

- learn stress-management techniques, including:

  ➢ Getting enough rest

  ➢ Slowing down and pace yourself

  ➢ Watching your "self-talk"

  ➢ Building your own support network

  ➢ Learning relaxation techniques

  ➢ Using laughter

EXERCISE

Regular exercise is nature's own antidepressant. Experts have found that exercise releases strong, natural mood lifters (called endorphins) that stay in the blood for hours. In addition to lifting your depression, exercise can:

- help you sleep better

- improve your concentration and memory

- burn excess pounds

- boost your self-esteem

- give you a feeling of greater control over your life and your condition

- help reduce any dependence on alcohol and drugs

If you have not been exercising regularly, check with your doctor first to make sure you don't have any health conditions that would keep you from doing certain activities. Follow these tips to make your exercise routine more successful and stress-reducing:

- Choose noncompetitive activities so you won't be making more stress.

- Use stretching or yoga to relax.

- Choose an activity or several activities you like and will stick with; vary your routine so you don't get bored.

- Select an aerobic exercise, one that makes you move your body and breathe deeply. Aerobic activities include:

  ➢ walking, jogging, or running

  ➢ biking (stationary or regular)

  ➢ rowing

  ➢ swimming

  ➢ cross-country skiing

  ➢ tennis, basketball, and other sports that need constant motion

  ➢ aerobic dance classes

- Start with just a few minutes and slowly increase your speed and distance.

- Begin and end with a few minutes of stretching and easy activity.

- Think about joining a gym. Some people find the ease and social aspect of a gym or exercise class motivating. It can also help you meet new friends and socialize, which is especially important if you tend to stay to yourself.

EAT HEALTHY FOODS

The saying goes, "You are what you eat." It might be more correct to say, "You feel what you eat." Many people find that food plays a big part in how they feel. For instance, some people say sugar makes them feel irritable or lethargic. Others say caffeine makes them anxious. Still others say alcohol or preservatives like monosodium glutamate (MSG) impact their moods. A healthful diet can help.

- **Eat a varied diet.** You'll get the nutrients you need if you eat from a wide menu. The easiest way to do this is to use the Food Guide Pyramid. The pyramid is a food system that automatically balances

Fats and Sweets—Sweets and fats can be added for extra calories. However, if you're having trouble digesting and absorbing fat, you may want to limit fat intake.

Dairy—(milk, yogurt, and cheese) 2–3 servings a day

Protein—(meat, poultry, fish, dried beans and peas, eggs, and nuts and seeds) 2–3 servings a day

Vegetables—3–5 servings a day

Fruits—2–4 servings a day

Grains—(bread, cereal, rice, and pasta) 6–11 servings a day

your nutrient mix. The key is to fill up on foods at the base of the pyramid: whole grains, fruits, and vegetables. Rich in vitamins and minerals, these foods have complex carbohydrates, an important low-fat energy source for the body.

• **Eat fresh, whole foods.** Highly processed foods are usually full of preservatives, sugar, sodium, and fat.

Learn Stress-Management Techniques

There are a number of ways you can prevent unnecessary stress and control your response to it. Every person feels stress uniquely, in response to different situations, and with different feelings. The ways you manage your stress in one situation may not be the same as those you use in another. Use this section to explore a variety of stress-management skills.

Get Enough Rest

Lack of sleep (or too much sleep) worsens depression and mania. The proper balance of rest and activity can help you prevent your mood disorder from coming back.

- **Go to bed and get up at the same time every day.** If you vary when you sleep and get up, it can throw off your body's internal clock, making it hard to sleep.

- **Don't exercise an hour or so before bed.** Regular exercise can help you sleep better, but exercising right before you go to bed can make it hard to fall asleep.

- **Cut down on caffeinated drinks.** They can leave you anxious and sleepless.

- **Start a good night routine.** A routine that includes activities like stretching, brushing your teeth, or drinking a cup of warm herbal tea tells your body it's time for sleep and helps you relax.

- **Cool off your bedroom.** You'll sleep better if your room is between 60 and 68 degrees.

- **Cut the light and the noise.** Your sleeping room should be dark and quiet. If you live where this isn't possible, think about using eye shades and ear plugs, or a white noise machine like a fan.

Slow Down and Pace Yourself

Sometimes feelings of depression can come from always having too little time and too much to do. This leaves us tired, overwhelmed, and drained by all the demands and conflicts. Don't fill your life so full that you're always busy and stressed. Try not to worry about the future. Instead, enjoy the moment. Time management skills can help you keep pace.

- Make a list of everything you want to do each day.

- Prioritize tasks and do the important ones when your energy is high and resources are there.

- Break tasks down into smaller steps.

- Match things that need to be done with the time left.

- Combine similar trips and tasks. For instance, make all outgoing phone calls in one session. Drive to the cleaners, the library, and the grocery store in one trip.

- Delegate as much as possible. Ask your co-workers, kids, partner, or roommate to take over some tasks.

- Reduce paperwork by handling each piece of paper only once. Throw away junk mail without opening it.

- Avoid time-wasters. If someone calls or drops by just to chat, arrange to talk later if you're busy.

- Throw potluck dinner parties instead of trying to do it all yourself.

- Be prepared. Mentally rehearse a stressful situation so you'll have a few options when the time comes. Gather any resources you'll need in advance.

- Ask for help. Admit when you have too many priorities.

- Learn to say no to requests for time when you already have enough to do.

- Slow down and think about one project at a time.

Watch Your "Self-Talk"

All of us bombard ourselves with an internal dialogue or "self-talk," in which we judge and comment on how we're doing. Listen to your internal sources of stress and depression.

- **Expectations for perfection.** We pressure ourselves by having expectations for our performance at work and at home that are not realistic. We want to be the perfect parent, caregiver, and employee all at once.

- **The need to do it all and have it all.** Society, through the media and role models, promotes our wanting to have it all and thinking that we can do it all. Few can really do this. This can set us up for feeling frustrated and sad.

- **Negative attitudes and feelings.** Attitudes are the way we look at our world. Do you choose to look at the stresses of balancing work and family life as problems, disasters, and crises, or as challenges, opportunities, and learning experiences? A healthy attitude puts events into perspective, letting us see them in different ways and sometimes letting us find positive or humorous aspects of change.

Begin to dispute your negative self-talk by asking yourself:

- Is there any rational support for this idea?

- What evidence do I have that this idea is true? False?

- What do I know about myself in other situations that tells me that my negative self-talk is wrong?

- Is there any evidence that my negative self-talk is true, or that I make myself suffer by telling myself to be unhappy?

- What is the worst thing that could *really* happen to me in this situation? How likely is that to happen?

If your self-talk makes you depressed, stop yourself and start substituting more positive statements.

- "I am powerless, a victim of chance." Substitute with "I am responsible and in control of my life."

- "I can't cope because this is too scary." Substitute with "I can learn to handle any scary situation if I take it slowly, one step at a time."

- "The world is a dangerous place." Substitute with "I can learn to become more comfortable with the outside world. I am excited at the opportunities the outside world can offer me."

- "I have to worry or the problem won't get better." Substitute with "Worrying doesn't change anything. Action changes things."

Build Your Own Support Network

You must create a support system to manage stress and depression successfully. Even if you choose not to take part in an organized self-help group, you can build and use the same kind of nurturing relationship with friends and loved ones. Some people think of it as a sign of weakness to ask others for help. Some cut themselves off in hard times. These people have the Lone Ranger syndrome—the idea that they have to deal with everything alone. But even the Lone Ranger had Tonto. From time to time, all of us can use the help of a support group. Do you know who makes up your support network?

Learn Relaxation Techniques

You can manage stress better by learning various relaxation techniques like **deep breathing**, **meditation**, and **progressive relaxation**, among others. Studies have found that regular, deep relaxation can enhance the effects of psychotherapy, lessen addiction to drugs, and reduce anxiety. For some people, relaxation techniques help lift them out of depression and let them feel more in control of their lives.

It's important to learn and practice whatever relaxation technique(s) you choose before you have an episode of depression or mania. Then, when a difficult episode comes on, you have a tool to cope. Classes on various relaxation techniques are usually given at community colleges, mental health agencies, or local hospitals. Video and audio tapes can be bought at book stores.

These basic elements are common to almost all relaxation techniques:

- **A mental device.** Use a secret sound, word or phrase (repeated silently or out loud) to clear your mind.

- **A passive attitude.** Ignore any thoughts that might distract you and focus your thoughts on the technique.

- **Decreased muscle tone.** Get in a comfortable position (in comfortable clothing, if possible) so that your muscles do little work.

- **A quiet environment.** Find a quiet place with few potential interruptions. Close your eyes while you practice the technique.

Try these relaxation techniques:

1. Abdominal breathing. Sit in a comfortable chair or lie down and place one hand on your stomach. Inhale through your nose slowly and deeply, filling up your stomach (your hand should move out). Then exhale slowly through your mouth. Push out all of the air, pulling your stomach in slightly. Repeat this cycle four to six times.

2. Meditation. This requires a quiet place where you won't be disturbed. There are a variety of techniques you can learn. With some, you focus your thoughts on an object such as a candle flame or your breath. Others use a "mantra," a word, sound, or phrase to direct your mind. Once you are comfortable in your quiet place, take a few deep breaths. Then silently repeat a word like "one" or "peace" three to four times per minute. Don't worry if thoughts or images come up. Turn your attention back to your breathing and your word, letting the thoughts float away. Start with five minutes of meditation twice a day. Build up to 15 to 20 minutes twice a day.

3. Progressive relaxation
This involves tensing and relaxing all the muscles in your body. Sit in a comfortable chair or lie flat on a comfortable surface in a quiet place where you won't be disturbed. Close your eyes. Starting at the top of your body and moving down, tense and then release muscles. Start with the muscles of your face— tense for a few seconds and then relax completely. Next, move to the muscles of the neck and shoulders, tensing and relaxing. Take time to notice the difference between how your muscle feels when it's tense and when it's relaxed. Move all the way down your body, tensing and relaxing.

Use Laughter

Studies show that laughter is good medicine. Besides being fun, there are physical benefits to laughter as well.

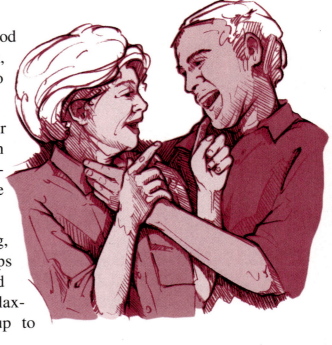

- Laughter exercises your lungs, increases oxygen in your circulatory system, and exercises the breathing muscles.

- After you stop laughing, your pulse rate drops below normal, and muscles relax. This relaxation effect can last up to 45 minutes.

- Laughter increases the production of endorphins—the body's natural mood lifters—just as exercise does.

When you're depressed, sometimes it's hard to find something to laugh about. Make a point of making laughter part of your life.

- Be playful, and let yourself have silly thoughts.

- Read the comic strips.

- Rent funny movies.

- Go out to a comedy club.

- Spend more time with friends or loved ones who have good senses of humor.

- Spread laughter to others. If you have funny thoughts, share them.

LIVING WITH DEPRESSION

Congratulations! You've just taken the first step in gaining control over your depression. By reading this book, you've empowered yourself with some of the latest information about your condition and you're ready to work with your health care team to win against your mood disorder.

GLOSSARY

A

Antidepressants
Medicines used to treat depression.

B

Behavioral therapy
A form of psychotherapy. It focuses on behaving in ways that bring satisfaction and happiness into your life, and changing those behaviors that don't.

Benefits
Insurance coverage for health care services.

Bipolar disorder
Episodes of mania, an excited state of heightened activity and euphoric or irritable feelings, followed by episodes of depression, periods of deep sadness and listlessness.

C

Cognitive therapy
A form of psychotherapy that focuses on changing thoughts or beliefs to improve mood. Often used successfully to treat depression.

D

Delusions
Fixed, false beliefs a person holds despite overwhelming evidence to the contrary. A grandiose delusion might be a person's belief that he or she was the next Christ.

Depression

A state of sadness or emotional uncaring that can be part of several mood disorders including major depression, bipolar disorder, dysthymia, and seasonal affective disorder.

Dysthymia

A chronic depression that can last for years. While it isn't as severe as a major depressive episode, the depression of dysthymia is more severe than just being down or feeling down in the dumps.

E

Electroconvulsive therapy (ECT)

Also known as "shock therapy," it is a technique used for severely depressed people in which a small electric current is sent into the brain.

Episode

An event or a time that is different than daily life. Specifically, a time that is characterized by symptoms of depression.

Euphoric mood

An exaggerated sense of well-being and contentment. Feeling expansive or elated. People with bipolar disorders often have euphoric moods during a manic episode.

F

Family therapy

Professional mental health therapy held with all members of the family, usually to resolve conflicts between spouses or between generations.

G

Group therapy

Professional mental health therapy in which a group of people with a similar problem or condition share their thoughts, feelings, and experiences with each other and with the therapist.

Hallucinations

False perceptions in hearing, seeing, touching, tasting, and smelling that aren't based on any external reality.

Heredity

The genetic process by which certain traits or conditions are passed from parent to child.

Hypersomnia

A pattern of too much sleeping.

Hypomania

A mild form of mania.

Individual therapy

Professional mental health therapy that is one on one between patient and therapist.

Insomnia

Trouble sleeping or inability to sleep.

Interpersonal therapy

A form of psychotherapy that focuses on fixing problems in current relationships.

Major depression

Also called clinical depression or simply depression, a major depressive episode is a medical disorder characterized by loss of interest in things one used to enjoy and feelings of sadness. Can also include physical symptoms such as headaches and other pain, digestive problems, and sexual troubles.

Mania

A time of extreme excitement and activity. Mania may involve extreme happiness, over-talkativeness, short attention span, and delusions about self-importance or personal powers.

Manic depression
See *Bipolar disorder.*

Mood disorders
A variety of mental conditions that all involve some periods of depression. They include major depression, bipolar disorder, dysthymia, and seasonal affective disorder.

N

Neuron
A single nerve cell.

Neurotransmitters
Chemicals in the brain that carry messages from one neuron to the next.

Norepinephrine
A natural hormone that increases blood pressure and elevates mood.

P

Postnatal
See *Postpartum.*

Postpartum
After childbirth.

Primary care provider (PCP)
The health care professional whom you see for routine care.

Psychotherapy
Any of several methods of treating mental and emotional disorders without medicines.

Receptor sites
Places on the surface of a cell where certain chemicals such as neurotransmitters attach to interact with the cell.

Referral
When a person is introduced to additional health care resources.

Re-uptake
The process by which a chemical neurotransmitter is absorbed into the neuron that released it before it can cross the synapse to the next neuron.

Seasonal affective disorder (SAD)
A mood disorder in which symptoms are seasonal—depression in the winter months, mania or hypomania in the spring and summer months.

Serotonin
One of many chemical neurotransmitters.

Side effect
Any reaction or consequence from a medicine or therapy.

Synapse
The area where two neurons meet, and across which nerve impulses are carried by neurotransmitters.

Therapist
A person with special skills in one or more areas of health care, especially mental health.

RESOURCES

For more information, including available books and pamphlets, and support groups in your area, contact any of these organizations:

National Alliance for the Mentally Ill (NAMI)
200 North Glebe Road, Suite 1015
Arlington, VA 22202-3754
800-950-6264

National Depressive and Manic Depressive Association (NDMDA)
730 North Franklin, Suite 501
Chicago, IL 60610
800-82-NDMDA

National Foundation for Depressive Illness, Inc. (NFDI)
P.O. Box 2257
New York, NY 10116-4344
800-248-4344

National Mental Health Association (NMHA)
National Mental Health Information Center
1021 Prince St.
Alexandria, VA 22314-2971
800-969-6642

Agency for Health Care Policy and Research (AHCPR) Publications
  Clearinghouse
P.O. Box 8547
Silver Spring, MD 20907
800-358-9295

Depression Awareness, Recognition, and Treatment (D/ART) Program
National Institute of Mental Health
5600 Fishers Lane, Room 10-85
Rockville, MD 20857
800-421-4211
301-433-4513

Depression and Related Affective Disorders Association (DRADA)
600 North Wolfe Street, Meyer 3-181
Baltimore, MD 21287-7381
410-955-4647
202-955-5800

Lithium Information Center
Dean Foundation
8000 Excelsior Drive, Suite 302
Madison, WI 53717-1914
608-836-8070

APPENDIX: QUESTIONS FROM THE DSM-IV

Is It Major Depression?

The DSM-IV lists these diagnostic criteria for major depression:

Five (or more) of the following symptoms present during the same two-week period. At least one of the symptoms is either 1) depressed mood or 2) loss of interest or pleasure.

1. Depressed mood most of the day, nearly every day (in children or adolescents, this can be an irritable mood).

2. Very little interest or pleasure in all or almost all activities on a daily basis.

3. Significant weight loss or gain when not dieting (a change of more than 5 percent of body weight in one month), or decrease in appetite on a daily basis (in children, failure to make expected weight gains).

4. Sleeplessness or hypersomnia (sleeping too much) every day.

5. Physical agitation or slowness on a daily basis.

6. Fatigue or loss of energy every day.

7. Feelings of worthlessness or excessive or inappropriate guilt nearly every day.

8. Lowered ability to think or concentrate, or indecisiveness on a daily basis.

9. Recurrent thoughts of death.

Is It Bipolar Disorder?

The DSM-IV lists these diagnostic criteria for a manic or hypomanic episode:

Manic Episode

1. A distinct period of abnormally and persistent elevated, expansive or irritable mood that lasts at least one week (or any duration if hospitalization is needed).

2. During the episode, three (or more) of the following symptoms persist (four if the mood is only irritable):

    • inflated self-esteem or grandiosity

    • less need for sleep (e.g. feeling rested after only three hours of sleep)

    • more talkative than usual or pressure to keep talking

    • flight of ideas or racing thoughts

    • easily distracted by unimportant factors

    • increase in activity (socially, at work or school, or sexually) or physical agitation

    • involvement in pleasurable activities that have a high potential for painful consequences (e.g. unrestrained buying sprees)

3. Mood disturbance is severe enough to impair work, social activities, or relationships with others, or need hospital care to keep the person from harming self or others.

4. Symptoms are not due to drug abuse, medicine or other treatment, or caused by a medical condition (e.g. hyperthyroidism).

Hypomanic Episode

1. Time of persistently elevated, expansive or irritable mood that lasts at least four days and is different from the usual nondepressed mood.

2. During the episode, three (or more) of the following symptoms persist:

    • inflated self-esteem

- less need for sleep (e.g. feeling rested after only three hours of sleep)

- more talkative than usual or pressure to keep talking

- flight of ideas or racing thoughts

- easily distracted by unimportant factors

- increase in activity (socially, at work or school, or sexually) or physical agitation

- involvement in pleasurable activities that have a high potential for painful consequences (e.g. unrestrained buying sprees)

3. Episode is linked with a noticeable change in functioning that is different from the person's normal behavior.

4. Mood change and disturbance is noticeable by others.

5. The episode isn't severe enough to cause serious impairment in work or social relations or need hospital care.

6. Symptoms are not due to drug abuse, medicine or other treatment, or caused by a medical condition (e.g. hyperthyroidism).

Is It Dysthymia?

The DSM-IV lists these diagnostic criteria for dysthymia, the chronic, milder form of depression:

1. Depressed mood for most of the day, more days than not, for at least two years (in children or adolescents, the mood can be irritable and must last at least one year).

2. While depressed, two (or more) of the following symptoms occur:

- poor appetite or overeating

- sleeplessness or hypersomnia

- low energy or fatigue

- low self-esteem

- poor concentration or difficulty making decisions

- feelings of hopelessness

3. During the two-year period (one year for children or adolescents), the person hasn't been without symptoms for more than two months at a time.

4. No major depression present during the first two years of the depression (one year for children or adolescents).

5. There has never been a manic, mixed, or hypomanic episode.

6. Disturbance isn't due to a chronic psychotic disorder like schizophrenia or delusional disorder.

7. Symptoms are not due to drug abuse, medicine or other treatment, or caused by a medical condition (e.g. hyperthyroidism).

8. Symptoms cause significant distress or problems in social, work, or other important areas.

SOURCES

Essential Psychopathology and Its Treatment, Jerrold S. Maxmen and Nicholas G. Ward, Norton and Co., New York, 1995.

The Consumer's Guide to Psychotherapy, Jack Engler, Ph.D., and Daniel Goleman, Ph.D., Simon and Schuster, New York, 1992.

Living Without Depression and Manic Depression, Mary Ellen Copeland, M.S., New Harbinger, Oakland, Calif., 1994.

The Depression Workbook: A Guide for Living With Depression and Manic Depression, Mary Ellen Copeland, M.S., New Harbinger, Oakland, Calif., 1992.

Handbook of Drug Therapy in Psychiatry, Jerrold G. Bernstein, PSG Publishing, Littleton, Mass. 1988.

Massachusetts General Hospital Handbook of General Hospital Psychiatry, Ned H. Cassem, M.D., Mosby Yearbook, St. Louis, 1991.

Depression in Late Life, Dan G. Blazer, M.D., Mosby Yearbook, St. Louis, 1993.

Geriatric Psychiatry and Psychopharmacology: A Clinical Approach, Michael A. Jenike, M.D., Mosby Yearbook, St. Louis, 1989.

The Handbook of Psychiatry, Barry Guze, M.D., ed., Yearbook Publishers, Chicago, 1990.

The Psychiatric Drug Handbook, Barry Guze, M.D., et al., Mosby Yearbook, St. Louis, 1992.

Alternative Medicine: The Definitive Guide, The Burton Goldberg Group, Future Medicine Publishing, Puyallup, Wash., 1993.

Surviving Grief and Learning to Live Again, Catherine M. Sanders, Ph.D., John Wiley and Sons, New York, 1992.

Personal Guide to Living With Loss, Elaine Vail, John Wiley and Sons, New York, 1982.

The Good News About Depression, Mark S. Gold, M.D., Bantam, New York, 1988.

Mood Disorders: Depression and Manic Depression, Demitri Papolos, M.D., National Alliance for the Mentally Ill, Arlington, Va..

Depression Is a Treatable Illness: A Patient's Guide, U.S. Department of Health and Human Services, Rockville, Md., 1993.

Depression in Primary Care, U.S. Department of Health and Human Services, Rockville, Md., 1993.

Depression in Primary Care: Detection, Diagnosis, and Treatment, U.S. Department of Health and Human Services, Rockville, Md., 1993.

NOTES

NOTES